DI

A
Weekend
with
Warren Buffett

A
WEEKEND
WITH
Warren Buffett

AND OTHER SHAREHOLDER
MEETING ADVENTURES

RANDY CEPUCH

THUNDER'S MOUTH PRESS
NEW YORK

A WEEKEND WITH WARREN BUFFETT
And Other Shareholder Meeting Adventures

Copyright © 2007 by Randy Cepuch

Published by
Thunder's Mouth Press
An Imprint of Avalon Publishing Group, Inc.
245 West 17th Street, 11th Floor
New York, NY 10011

AVALON
publishing group incorporated

First printing, August 2006

Names of some nonpublic figures have been changed to protect their privacy. Dialogue may be inexact because most companies prohibit use of recording devices at shareholder meetings. Facts and fugures used are typically those that were current when events described were held.

Library of Congress Cataloging-in-Publication Data is available.

ISBN-10: 1-56025-954-X
ISBN-13: 978-1-56025-954-1

9 8 7 6 5 4 3 2 1

Book design by Maria Fernandez

Printed in the United States of America
Distributed by Publishers Group West

To Nancy

CONTENTS

INTRODUCTION

Every spring, I spend a weekend with Warren Buffett. He tells me what he thinks of the world these days, provides me with my annual dose of common sense, and sends me on my way. In general, it's an exercise that helps to keep me out of serious trouble as an investor.

Oh, it's not just Warren and me. There are twenty thousand or so other people. We're all investors in Berkshire Hathaway, and we're in Omaha for the company's shareholder meeting festivities. As Berkshire's CEO and chairman of the board, Buffett—who is widely considered to be the world's smartest living investor and one of the most ethical businessmen on the planet—takes on any and all questions for more than six hours. He riffs on life, love, and accounting, among other things, and makes sure everyone feels welcome. When a shy woman prefaces her query apologetically, noting that she owns just one share, Buffett offers encouragement by observing that he is her partner and that between the two of them they own the largest part of the company.

I began making my annual visits to Omaha in 1999— the right time to hear Buffett's prescient cautions about the "here today, gone tomorrow" fortunes of Internet and technology companies, and the warnings rang true to me.

As it happened, I owned shares in a few of those companies. Several years earlier, I had invested in some limited partnerships—basically, contributed small amounts

to pools of money doled out by venture capitalists backing
high-risk startup companies. It's not unusual for most or
even all of the startups to go bust, but the idea is that a few
will do well and the investors in the partnership will
receive what are essentially founders' shares. I was lucky.
My partnerships caught the technology wave—that
amazing period where it seemed any sort of business with
an Internet tie-in could issue shares and watch their price
go up tenfold overnight. Suddenly I started receiving
modest distributions of shares in companies that I'd never
heard of before—companies whose names sounded like
what the Jetsons might call their cat.

Until then my experiences with the stock market had
been almost entirely indirect. Since the early 1980s, I'd
been writing annual reports and the like for American
Funds, one of the nation's largest and most successful
mutual fund groups. Not surprisingly, I had opted to put
my own money in mutual funds—which are, of course,
portfolios of stocks that someone else chooses.[1] Even in
all my years of writing about funds and reading the business press, I'd rarely gotten to know any individual company very well.

Except for Berkshire Hathaway, that is. I had long been
an admirer of the plainspoken and unassuming Buffett and

---

[1]Mutual funds offer broad diversification and professional management, so they can be very good investments for many people. Yet funds
have seldom done a very good job of educating shareholders about
the companies they own, indirectly, through their investments. The
problem worsened in 2004, when the Securities and Exchange
Commission decided that funds didn't need to identify, in published
portfolios, any companies that weren't among the fifty largest holdings
(or that represented less than 1% of a fund's assets). Of course, those
"little" holdings can add up and before you know it, a third or more of
a portfolio can be listed, quite unhelpfully, as "Other."

his company, a conglomerate including interests so diverse that some investors persist in thinking of it as a mutual fund all by itself. Most of Berkshire's holdings—businesses like insurance underwriters and shoe manufacturers— aren't very sexy, so the company's share price was slipping in the late 1990s as investors deserted the "old economy" and rushed off into tech and dot-com stocks. I'd learned just enough about investing over the years to know that it was often effective to buck the herd, especially if the stampede didn't seem to make any sense. I bought a single share in Berkshire Hathaway—my first individual stock purchase—and at the first opportunity I headed for Omaha to take in the shareholder meeting.

As I listened to Buffett's dire predictions for Internet and technology stocks, I realized that I knew dangerously little about the companies whose shares had been turning up in my mailbox. Most of them seemed to be involved in "solutions optimization aggregation processes" or similar mumbo jumbo—things I was convinced I would never understand.

So I started selling those stocks and investing the proceeds in the stocks of well-established companies whose businesses *did* make sense to me, often due to my first-hand experiences or those of family and friends. Before long, I'd put together a modest portfolio of individual stocks that more or less reflected my personal beliefs and interests, as portfolios often do. I did my best, for example, to avoid companies that abused animals, operated nuclear power plants, or had Dan Quayle on their board of directors.

When I decided to hang up my corporate hat in 2001, I became more dependent on my investments and began to wonder if I really knew "my" companies.

Attending Berkshire's shareholder meetings had opened my eyes to what I could learn. Might the annual events put on by other companies have something to offer to an individual investor like me? And how might they compare to Berkshire's "Woodstock of Capitalism"? I decided to see how companies treated me on the one day of the year they're required to fling open the doors and let all the owners inside for a peek—whether they want to or not.

Over the next five years, I went to more than fifty shareholder meetings in the United States, Europe, and Australia. All of those trips involved plenty of planes, trains, and automobiles and helped ease what otherwise might have been an abrupt transition from decades of business travel. They also got me out of the house often enough that my wife, Nancy, was spared the shock of suddenly having me around all the time.

During my quest, I met beloved and beleaguered business bigwigs, learned that shareholder democracy is pretty much a myth, and enjoyed an occasional free lunch. Sometimes I saw or heard things that led me to sell my shares—or, less frequently, to buy more. Along the way, my curiosity grew to the point where I bought a few stocks just to be able to attend potentially interesting meetings (not a practice I would recommend)!

In *A Weekend with Warren Buffett*, I'll take you to several annual corporate gatherings and tell you what goes on—both the usual and the unusual, with an emphasis on the latter. My hope is that these vicarious visits will encourage you to learn more about your own investments (or perhaps to become an investor) and help you decide if and when it might be worthwhile to try sticking your nose under a corporate tent.

AN IMPORTANT P.S.: In this book I'll tell you a bit about how and why I came to own certain stocks. But please don't make investment decisions based solely on what I've written about the companies discussed. You should always do your own homework—called "due diligence" on Wall Street. After all, my reports are snapshots, and it's safe to assume there's an element of corporate kabuki involved in many shareholder meetings. In any case, the companies, the characters, and the world have all changed since—sometimes dramatically. (Humorist Will Rogers captured the challenge nicely when he suggested, "Buy good quality common stocks and hold 'em until they go up. If they don't go up, don't buy 'em.")

1

Off to See the Wizard
BERKSHIRE HATHAWAY

Disclosure: I have long savored the candid and informative annual report letters penned by Warren Buffett, CEO and chairman of the board of Berkshire Hathaway. Many of his admirers call him "The Wizard of Omaha." To me, he's the business world's equivalent of Captain Kangaroo—smart, amusing, moral, and beloved. Berkshire Hathaway is a unique conglomeration of businesses owned outright (from GEICO to Dairy Queen) and large holdings in other corporations (from Coca-Cola to American Express). It's the first individual stock I ever purchased.

Well before dawn on the first Saturday in May, there's a long line of the faithful wrapped around Omaha's largest arena. You would think, perhaps, that they were queued in hopes of scoring some tickets to a just-announced Bruce Springsteen concert. Truth is, they're here to see a marathon performance by a very different legend—the septuagenarian hero of the investment world, Warren Buffett.

For more than six hours later today (including a lunch break), Buffett will munch candies and drink Cherry Cokes while entertaining and educating some twenty thousand people at Berkshire Hathaway's annual share-holder meeting. It's the highlight of an extraordinary weekend of events collectively known as the "Woodstock of Capitalism." (Ironically, the generation best repre-sented in the audience is the very one that smoked joints and rolled in the mud in Max Yasgur's pasture a month after man walked on the moon.)

Buffett shares the stage with vice chairman Charlie Munger. Ostensibly, the two are here to take questions related to Berkshire Hathaway. But the reality is that the shareholders, guests, and media present have come to see what the Wizard, aka "The Oracle of Omaha," has to say about bigger issues. Buffett is widely considered to be the closest thing American business has to a conscience and is often called the world's best investor. He's unquestionably one of the most successful: only Bill Gates, his occasional bridge partner (and, as of 2005, a member of Berkshire's board of directors) has more money.

Not surprisingly, multitudes make the pilgrimage to Omaha each year, hoping some of Buffett's famous investment acumen and impeccable ethical standards will rub off.

I join them for the first time in 1999, and my debut shareholder meeting experience gets off to a very unlikely start: Half an hour after arriving, I stumble into the Wizard himself. It's the equivalent of running into a famous guru at the base camp on the night before you plan to climb the mountain.

Fresh off the plane, I stop by Aksarben ("Nebraska" spelled backward) Coliseum, an aging sports arena where the meeting is to take place the next day. Outside the building there's a display by Executive Jet, a private airplane leasing company owned by Berkshire. As I'm talking with the hostess at the display, she smiles and says, "Oh, here comes Mr. Buffett." Sure enough, Buffett emerges from behind the wheel of his Lincoln Town Car. He strides over, alone, brushes back a shock of unruly white hair, energetically shakes hands with the half dozen of us present, chats a bit, and poses for a few pictures. I'm so startled by his accessibility that I don't have the presence of mind to do anything other than thank him for doing such a good job. (It reminds me of how I reacted when I met Linda Ronstadt after a concert in the 1970s, but with less drool.)

As I drive to my hotel, it's obvious that Omaha merchants adore the first weekend in May. There are signs everywhere welcoming Berkshire shareholders. Yet many of the people attending the meeting are locals who've been Berkshire investors for decades; there are plenty of unassuming millionaires who call Omaha home.

For those who come from afar, it's essential to make air and hotel reservations early. Six months beforehand isn't a bad idea. Wait too long and you risk being shut out. Still, there's the matter of the all-important credentials. Shareholders get theirs by returning a postcard included in the annual report, mailed in late March. Others can either try to tag along with a shareholder (who can request up to four credentials) or buy credentials on eBay (where Berkshire itself offers the passes at a low fixed price, hoping to minimize scalping). The badges-on-strings are accompanied by visitor guides that include the weekend schedule, directions and transportation details, and a list of hotels, restaurants, and a few area attractions.

In April 2002 the travel section of the *Washington Post* ran a short piece that began, "Three words you'll probably never hear: Welcome to Omaha." It went on to describe a few things worth seeing or doing should you somehow accidentally end up in what the writer regarded as the nation's bellybutton. A few weeks later I was in Omaha when that city's *World-Herald* noted the *Post*'s dig. In typical Midwestern fashion, the Nebraska paper resisted the impulse to sling a well-deserved meadow muffin at Washington. (It's ironic that the *Post* took a slap at Omaha, because Buffett spent part of his childhood ambitiously juggling five newspaper routes in the Washington area—including a *Post* route. What's more, Berkshire Hathaway owns approximately 18 percent of the Washington Post Company, and Buffett currently serves as lead director of the *Post*'s board.)

Despite the *Post*'s put-down, there's plenty to keep Berkshire Hathaway meeting attendees busy in Omaha. If checking out the house where former president Gerald Ford was born isn't enough, there are special shareholderonly sales at Berkshire-owned Nebraska Furniture Mart and Borsheim's Jewelry, both among the largest of their species anywhere. There's a bash at a local Dairy Queen where shareholders can lick free cones while getting Berkshire-related books signed by the authors and sometimes Buffett himself. There are informal receptions, some sponsored by Berkshire companies and others by fan clubs.

The heart of the weekend, though, is the meeting itself. Most such gatherings last an hour or two; Berkshire's takes up most of a day. The doors open at 7:00 a.m. on Saturday and there's a frenzied rush for good seats. More than a few copies of the distinctly peach-colored *Financial Times* distributed free outside the building are placed over chairs to stake turf claims, enabling shareholders to grab a little breakfast and check out the exhibition hall before the meeting begins.

From early morning until late afternoon, many of the companies owned wholly or in large part by Berkshire host booths in the exhibitor area. Visitors are greeted with tasty samples from See's Chocolates, a hugely successful West Coast subsidiary.

Nearly all the booths offer a freebie of one sort or another. Among the more noteworthy in recent years: copies of the Beatles' *Revolver* CD (which includes "Taxman") from H&R Block, teddy bears from Benjamin Moore Paints, Rubik's cubes from Shaw Industries, foldable binoculars from Johns Manville, and Olympic pins and commemorative bottles from Coca-Cola. (Of course, you can *buy* stuff, too—everything from a lollipop to part ownership in one of those executive jets—not to mention shoes, vacuum cleaners, encyclopedias, Oriental rugs, diamond bracelets, and even designer Christmas tree ornaments featuring Berkshire's charmingly tacky logo: a fistful of dollars.)

Meanwhile, there are photo ops tied to Berkshire subsidiaries. You can have your picture taken with the bushel of costumed characters that starred in Fruit of the Loom's TV commercials, or with GEICO's gecko. At Dairy Queen's booth you can capture forever the precious moment when you stood next to someone dressed as an ice cream cone.

Back in the auditorium, the program begins at 8:30 with a Berkshire home movie put together by Buffett's daughter, Susie. It's an hour-long hodgepodge of clips featuring Buffett doing everything from testifying before Congress to singing show tunes while accompanying himself on ukulele.

Many clips appear year after year, but there's always new material—often involving a celebrity cameo or two. One popular skit features Buffett and Bill Gates appearing before Judge Judy. She refers to Buffett as an "elderly delinquent" and tells Gates to "go to shutup.com." Cartoon shorts by an Omaha animator feature Buffett, Munger, and various Berkshire company product placements in parodies of a James Bond movie, *I Love Lucy*, and *Wayne's World*.

The 2003 segment included a takeoff on *The Wizard of Oz*, featuring Buffett (as Dorothy) and Munger (as Toto) lost in Kansas after a tornado. Bill Gates was the wizard who got them back to Omaha. (Coincidentally, there was a real twister the next day, and I spent several hours in the shelter of the basement at a local museum where the grocery store once operated by Buffett's uncle, grandfather, and great-grandfather was a featured exhibit.)

Often the film salutes companies that are new to the Berkshire stable. When Fruit of the Loom was acquired, Buffett taped a fake interview with CNBC's Ron Insana, revealing both a potential slogan—"We cover the asses of the masses"—and the reason for the purchase: "For years, Charlie's been saying we need to get into women's under-wear. Charlie's seventy-eight. It's now or never."

Over the years, the film has featured several variations on the 1971 "I'd Like to Teach the World to Sing" Coke ad. The original commercial segues into awkward follow-the-bouncing-ball references to Berkshire companies such as the *Buffalo News* and various insurance subsidiaries: "The presses run / we've bet a ton / on a super-catastrophe." (Hmmm. I'm hoping they actually bet *against* one of those!)

Occasionally the film returns to Warren himself, still strumming along on his ukulele. Each time he appears, he's playing in a different part of the arena, finishing in the men's room, where the last sound is that of a toilet flushing. All in all, it's a humble and endearing performance.

The official business meeting—perhaps the least inter-esting thing that happens all weekend—doesn't take long.

Because Buffett owns roughly 40 percent of the company's shares, votes tend to be foregone conclusions, and he's typically able to dispense with the agenda very quickly.

The basic formalities are the same at pretty much any shareholder meeting: The secretary certifies that a quorum is present in person or represented by votes cast in advance, the directors are introduced, nominations are made for election or reelection to the board, the auditor is introduced, shareholders vote on the directors and perhaps the auditor, and the business meeting is adjourned. Sometimes there's a bit more—perhaps a complicated executive compensation plan or two (which the company strongly encourages you to support) or maybe a proposal by a shareholder who is interested in saving the world in one way or another (which in most cases the company strongly encourages you to oppose). Berkshire's meetings tend to be simple—in part because for the past twenty-five years, Buffett has been content to work for a very modest one-hundred-thousand-dollar salary. It's safe to say he doesn't really need the money.

Upon wrapping up the required proceedings, Buffett and Munger open a can of See's peanut brittle and Buffett announces, "We'll be here for six hours or until the candy runs out." (Despite the epic proportions of the event, Buffett says, "Charlie and I don't spend a minute preparing for the meeting and sometimes don't even see each other earlier in the weekend except across the room at a dinner he holds on Friday night.")

Munger is another Omaha native who has done okay for himself. He's a lawyer, seven years older than Buffett. He lives in Los Angeles and pursues a wide variety of interests— reading voraciously about nearly everything, working with charities he holds near and dear, and running Wesco

Financial, a steel/banking/furniture rental conglomerate that is 80 percent owned by Berkshire.

He's a stiff presence—there's a running gag about replacing him with a life-size cardboard cutout—and Buffett usually chides Munger by introducing him as a "hyperkinetic bundle of energy." Often, when Munger is prompted for comments by Buffett, he'll simply say, "Nothing to add." When he does have something to say, though, it's well worth a listen.

A few days after the Berkshire gathering each year, Munger holds court at Wesco's shareholder meeting in Pasadena, California. The difference between the two meetings is pronounced: Buffett isn't present at Wesco's, so Munger does pretty much all the talking. Also, Wesco's low-key gathering draws just a few hundred shareholders or interested folks (no credentials were necessary when I attended in 2000), and there are no sideshows.

The audience here in Omaha doesn't look like a United Nations assembly, but it's far more diverse than most other shareholder gatherings, and quite a few of the world's major countries are represented. Although it's a Saturday, some shareholders are wearing business clothes. Perhaps 30 percent of the crowd is women, and there are more than a few children on hand. It's a well-heeled bunch, by definition: Because Buffett doesn't believe in stock splits, shares cost thousands of dollars each (as of mid-2006, class A shares cost approximately ninety thousand dollars and class B shares ran about three thousand dollars). Some shareholders read, some knit, but most pay rapt attention, hanging on every word from Buffett and Munger.

Microphones are located at stations throughout the auditorium and in the overflow space, where shareholders who didn't arrive in time watch the proceedings on video screens. Buffett simply calls on each station in sequence and does his best to keep things moving.

It's not easy. Until 2004, when Buffett implemented a "one per customer" rule, there were always a few smarmy show-offs who would begin with "Just three quick questions," each of which somehow involved obscure acronyms and complex calculations. They were pretty impressed with themselves and clearly trying to stump the master; Buffett would have none of it. He gently deflated the questioners, then translated the questions into plain English and answered them in ways Average Joes and Janes would understand. Buffett seems unflappable and has more facts and figures stored away in his brain than any audience could exhaust.

He and Munger savor the exchanges with their fellow shareholders. "We like the idea of shareholders behaving like owners. Too often they behave like sheep," Buffett says.

Some questions seem to be perennials:

- *How are you feeling these days?* Buffett—in his mid-seventies—invariably responds by saying he tap dances to work each day, that he loves his work and the people he works with, that there's zero stress in his job.

- *What happens to Berkshire Hathaway when you die?* Buffett jests that he's left strict orders: "The first thing they should do is take my pulse again." He explains that his role will be divided among several people; whom they'll be depends on when he passes away. He acknowledges that the stock price will take a hit upon his demise but insists that will probably make it a great day to buy shares.

- *Why doesn't Berkshire invest more aggressively?* Buffett has famously avoided technology stocks and says Berkshire won't invest in companies he doesn't understand: "We look for things with durable competitive advantage and good management." (In 1999 he admitted, "If I had to bet, I'd bet heavily on Microsoft. But I don't have to bet. We are willing to trade away a big payoff for a certain payoff.") Munger has also been known to weigh in against taking unnecessary risks, asking why anyone who is already comfortably well off would care if someone else was getting richer faster.

- *What do you think about the stock market?* Buffett says, "I don't think about the market. We look at individual businesses. We don't think of stocks as things that wiggle in the paper every day; we think of stocks as parts of businesses." He often adds, "The stock market closes on Saturdays and Sundays and I don't break out in hives."

- *What's a reasonable rate of return to expect from stocks?* Buffett always tries to keep expectations reasonable, and in recent years he's said to look for 6 to 7 percent.

- *What should adults teach children?* "Tell them they only get one mind and one body," Buffett says. "Take care of and maximize both, so that when they're fifty, sixty, seventy, they'll have a real asset. Your main asset is yourself. Develop, maintain, and enhance it."

- *What financial advice would you give a child?* "Don't start out behind the eight ball. It's so hard to get out of debt. Stay away from credit cards," Buffett advises.

- *How do you become a successful investor?* Buffett offers, "Have a philosophy and don't be greedy. Insulate yourself from popular opinion. You're better off sitting and thinking about business characteristics and potential earnings. Read lots of annual reports."

- *How do you become successful, period?* Buffett answers, "I've had terrific role models and they've never let me down. You copy those people. Pick out the person you most admire . . . and ask, why can't I be like that?" Munger, a big fan of Ben Franklin, adds, "There's no reason to look at just the living. Some of the best role models have been dead a long time."

- *How would you define success?* "If all you do is achieve wealth by passively holding bits of paper, you will have a failed life," Buffett cautions. "When you get to be my age, you will be successful if the people you hope would love you do love you. It's something you can't buy. The way to be loved is to be lovable. You always get back more than you give."

Berkshire's own annual report letters typically include sermons on business world practices that Buffett finds lacking, and the topics are explored in depth during the Q&A. Often the focus is on stupid accounting tricks. Buffett says, "We deplore solving operating problems by using accounting maneuvers."

Among other things, that means he opposes abuse of stock options as executive compensation. He calls options—which are essentially rights to buy shares at less than the market price—"lottery tickets" and has long insisted that their costs should be included prominently in expenses shown in company reports. (Effective in 2006 he got his wish.) Munger, on the same bandwagon, observes, "Stock options for older executives—sixty plus—are immoral. People that age are already loyal."

Then there are the unrealistic expectations some companies have for the funds designated to pay pensions to their retirees. Munger says that expecting to meet pension liabilities by assuming unlikely returns is "like living on an earthquake fault and saying the longer it's been without an earthquake, the lower the chances."

Neither Buffett nor Munger have much good to say about using derivatives—contracts whose ultimate values often depend on things like interest rates and weather conditions, which can lead to wild fluctuations and bookkeeping shenanigans. Munger doesn't hold back: "To say that derivative accounting is a sewer is an insult to sewage."

And they warn that investors should be wary of fraud at companies reporting "EBITDA" results—Earnings Before Interest, Taxes, Depreciation, and Amortization (or, put another way, Everything But Items That Definitely Affect value!). Munger says, "Anytime you see the words 'EBITDA earnings,' you should substitute 'bullshit earnings.'"

Munger is known for getting off at least one such zinger every meeting—typically sometime after the half-hour lunch break. Truth is, it's a good idea to have a pen and paper handy all day, because you never know when he or Buffett will serve up a pithy observation. Sometimes you don't even need to know the context to appreciate the remark.

- "'Can you sell it?' is not an adequate moral test," rules Munger.

■ "Humans are best at interpreting information so that all prior conclusions remain intact," observes Buffett. (In a similar vein: "What we learn from history is that people don't learn from history.")

■ "If you mix raisins with turds, they're still turds," pronounces Munger.

■ "The trick in building a big snowball is to start at the top of the hill," advises Buffett.

There's also plenty of sound business advice. Some of it is anything but intuitive. For instance, Buffett says progress isn't necessarily good for investors: "We view change as more of a threat than an opportunity. We look for the absence of change to protect ways that are already making money. We like to see something that looks like it'll be very much the same ten years from now."

Of course, there's typically more than a bit of banter about Berkshire companies. When a shareholder asks about the seismic risks that Berkshire faces as the largest insurer in California, Buffett precedes his real answer with "My sister in Carmel calls when the dogs and cats start running in circles."

Sometimes the cheerleading for Berkshire company products seems to be overkill. Talking up the shareholders-only sale at Borsheim's Jewelry, Munger says, "When you're buying jewelry for the woman you love, it probably shouldn't get too much financial consideration." Buffett adds, "I've never bought a piece of jewelry where I've regretted the outcome."

Of course, onsite sales no doubt at least help to cover the cost of the whole extravaganza. In any case, humility always wins out. Buffett frequently points out that the odds are overwhelmingly against his ability to do better in the future than he has in the past (after all, $10,000 invested with him in 1956 has grown to more than $500 *million!*). Also, he knows it's a good idea to remind investors that he and Munger are far from infallible. When a slide appears on a screen behind the two men, showing a line graph indicating tremendous growth, Buffett announces it represents Blue Chip Stamps, an early Berkshire holding—*and that it's upside down.*

There is, Buffett readily concedes, a certain degree of luck behind his success: "It wouldn't have happened if I'd been born in Bangladesh, or two hundred years ago." As a result, he says he pays his taxes gladly and feels it's unfair to cut taxes for the wealthy. He's even written an opinion piece for the *Washington Post*, criticizing Bush administration proposals that would result in Buffett paying only *one-tenth* the percentage in taxes that his secretary pays. Asked why he seldom does such things, Buffett replies, "There's something very unattractive about a rich guy who pops his mouth off a lot."

Around 3:30 Buffett and Munger wrap things up. Berkshire's shareholders head out to explore Omaha and mull over the Wizard's words. I find myself simultaneously refreshed and exhausted. As I digest what I've heard and seen, I realize that what Buffett does must be quite rare. After all, how many top executives would really let people see the man behind the curtain, the way he's so willing to do?

It seems unlikely that any other meeting of corporate shareholders could cover so much ground or teach investors as much. But after one of my early trips to Omaha, I wonder if other gatherings might offer rewards of their own. I decide to find out. That fall, when a proxy statement and shareholder meeting notice arrives from a certain coffee company, I decide to accept the invitation.

Oddly enough, the place where I'm headed calls itself the Emerald City.

In a nutshell . . .

BERKSHIRE HATHAWAY

EDUCATIONAL VALUE: **A+**
An immersion course in business . . . and more.

ENTERTAINMENT VALUE: **A**
Hour-long film, various sideshows.

FREEBIES: **A**
Cokes, Rubik's cubes, binoculars, CDs, etc.

FOOD & DRINK: **C**
Arena concessions offer little variety.

INSIGHT: Warren Buffett fans have called Berkshire Hathaway's annual shareholder meeting "an MBA in a day." That's because the legendary all-day Q&A sessions feature two extremely bright men—Buffett and Charlie Munger—holding forth not just on details about the company, but about business and the world in general. It's like sitting on the porch with two kindly grandfathers, both eager to help you succeed beyond your wildest dreams. There's truly something for everyone here, and it's a safe bet that every attendee—whether a professional portfolio manager or a child who makes money mowing lawns—learns how to be a better investor (and maybe even a better human).

Whole Latté Love
STARBUCKS

Disclosure: I've never been much of a coffee drinker, and even now I don't understand why espresso machines can't be fitted with mufflers. But I've long noted the devotion of Starbucks patrons and admired how well the company seems to do almost everything. In 1999 opportunity knocked when the company's stock price seemed inexplicably decaffeinated.

S tarbucks' familiar logo, a green circle with a stylized mermaid in the middle, punctuates the urban landscape in many parts of America—but nowhere more than Seattle. After all, this is a city where it's not unusual to see a street vendor in the middle of a block dispensing steaming cups to java junkies unable to make it as far as one of the coffee shops on either corner. So it's hardly surprising that there's a Starbucks across the street from Benaroya Hall, in the heart of downtown. Nor is it surprising that there's a Starbucks outlet in the outer perimeter of the venue itself.

What *is* surprising is that on the morning of Starbucks' 2002 shareholder meeting, caffeine-craving investors who could drink all they want *for free* in the Benaroya lobby choose to patronize those stores, instead—and *pay full price* for their fixes! I watch for a while before I understand: the lines are (somewhat) shorter at the stores!

So what if there are crews of Starbucks associates wandering around the lobby with scuba-style coffee tanks strapped to their backs, filling mugs like keg minders at a frat party? And *so what* if giving the barista across the street the business means having to run a gauntlet of anti-Starbucks protesters wandering around out front? (Do my eyes deceive me, or are some of those very protesters waking up with go-juice obtained behind enemy lines?) All in all, it's a heartwarming reassurance that Starbucks is right on track with what I have long suspected is the company's plan to take over the world.

On the sidewalk, the picketers are gathering for a 10:30 rally against genetically modified foods. Somebody may have goofed with the planning, because that's a half hour *after* the shareholder meeting will get under way. By 9:45 only a dozen or so protesters are on site, as an equal number of Seattle police officers watch nearby, on horseback.

Considering the presence of hostile forces, security seems a little lax at the door. Nobody asks me for proof of share ownership or even for any identification, although a smiling Starbucks representative asks me to fill out a card indicating whether I'm a shareholder. It doesn't seem as if a "no" answer would get me thrown out of the party.

My fellow shareholders are more diverse than I had expected. Somehow I'd figured that people who would come to annual meetings held on weekdays would tend to be older men or couples, retirees with flexible schedules. But the Starbucks crowd—some three thousand strong— is different. It skews younger. Or maybe it just seems that way because everyone's so damned alert.

The perks begin immediately. Just past the entrance are huge piles of the day's *New York Times*, free for meeting attendees. More important, there's breakfast. At least a half dozen tables are heaped with pastries—thousands of muffins, scones, and similarly naughty and delicious morning snacks meant to complement the oceans of exotic bean broth being consumed all around me. In addition to the roving latté sprayers, there are coffee stations, espresso stations, even tea stations. I rarely drink coffee. When everyone around me is getting wired, I'm the designated yawner. An hour from now, I'll probably be one of the few people in the building not searching for a bathroom.

Oddly, no food or beverages are allowed in the auditorium where the actual meeting will take place. Predictably, this causes a major traffic jam, and more than a few shareholders opt to stay in the lobby, sipping their double half-caffs, scarfing blueberry muffins, and watching the proceedings on closed-circuit monitors. It's just as well, because before long nearly all the seats are full.

Inside the auditorium, the stage is a pseudo rain forest, strewn with coffee bags and plantation props plus a few comfortable couches. Quichua Mashis—a serape-wrapped bunch, playing guitars, panpipes, and hand drums—is making ethereal new-ageish "Music from the Andes" and looking mystified both by the surroundings and the crowd.

The first ten rows of seats are taped off, presumably for the Wall Street muckety-mucks, who tend to be more equal than other investors at such gatherings. Most of the reserved area is still empty when the band finishes its set to polite applause, nearly fifteen minutes after the meeting's scheduled start time. As the lights go down, I watch as a woman sneaks her forbidden cup of coffee past the ushers and quickly takes a seat in the off-limits section.

A short, slick video kicks things off, featuring two Seattle sports stars lauding forty-eight-year-old founder and chairman Howard Schultz as "the man who makes it all happen." Their celebrity is pretty much lost on anyone who is not a Seattle resident or a sports fan, but never mind. What's important is that the video establishes Schultz as a hero.

Then Schultz himself takes the stage, wearing a suit that probably cost as much as six hundred cappuccinos. He nods and scowls simultaneously, like an earnest Kevin Nealon delivering the "Weekend Update" news on an old episode of *Saturday Night Live*. The crowd roars. For many in the audience, Schultz isn't just the guy who runs the company they invest in, he's also the boss of the company where they work.

Immediately, Schultz strikes a humble note, invoking "our commitment to origin countries" and explaining that the Latin American warm-up band shows how Starbucks is looking out for the places where the beans come from. He adds a few words about the tragedies of September 11 before introducing a gospel choir to sing "America the Beautiful." The song, he says, applies to everyone in the world. It's merely the first odd geographic assertion of the day.

While the choir exits, Schultz introduces the corporate directors, then asks all the Starbucks associates in the crowd to stand—and suddenly it's clear why there are so many younger people present. They're all baristas!

During the next few minutes, Schultz says all the right things for employees and shareholders alike. "Can a company get big but stay small?" he asks, observing that the company has grown from one hundred stores in 1992 (when its stock was first publicly traded) to some five thousand stores in twenty-six countries a decade later, serving some twenty million customers each week. It doesn't surprise me a bit when he concludes that Starbucks can indeed get big but still feel like a small company—and that it's in the process of doing just that. (A pal who speaks fluent Starbucks lingo tells me later that the question really should've been, "Can the company get *venti* but stay *tall?*")

Next, for investors who are unnerved by headlines about corporate accounting scandals: "This company's balance sheet and accounting practices are above reproach."

Then a real crowd-pleaser: "Starbucks is in the *people* business." That's a typical corporate claim, to be sure—but Schultz makes a strong case by pointing out that Starbucks was the first public company to give part-timers health benefits and stock options. Everyone around me beams.

Schultz's pep talk is capped by a ceremony high-lighting the countries where the company does business. Employees tote the appropriate flags down the aisles and across the stage as the list of nations scrolls slowly on the video screens. Problem: Shanghai and Hawaii are *not* countries. A company bent on world domination prob-ably ought to have a better handle on geography. Oh, well. (Later I discover that the company's annual report places Hawaii in *Latin America*. I contact their investor relations department and am told "that's just the way we divide it up internally." Residents of the fiftieth state, consider yourselves warned: Learn Spanish pronto, so you'll be prepared when Starbucks officially starts calling the shots.)

Off to one side, an interpreter turns Schultz's remarks into sign language for the benefit of any deaf attendees. It's a very thoughtful gesture. (I suspect it's far more effective than closed-caption translations. At Walgreen's shareholder meeting in 2006, captions appearing onscreen shortly after the words were spoken were surprisingly accurate at first. After a while, though, it became clear that was probably because the scripted stuff was pre-typed and the off-the-cuff material wasn't—which led to amusingly cryptic messages such as "There were 1BLIRKS.")

A video follows, interspersing bits of appearances Schultz has made on CNBC with footage from movies such as *Best in Show*. The idea is to poke fun at how the company seems to turn up everywhere. Interestingly, one place where Starbucks *isn't* is in Schultz's hands: after he introduces CEO Orin Smith, he sits down on one of the couches and sips from *a glass of water.*

Smith offers up a cliché: "Our greatest potential still lies ahead." He says the prospects in North America are "enormous"—Montana, Alaska, North Dakota, South Dakota, Nebraska, Iowa, Arkansas, and West Virginia are, as of this writing, virgins—and that business outside North America "will exceed even that."

During the previous twelve months, Smith says, the company opened more than twelve hundred stores. In the year to come, he announces, Starbucks will set up shop in Germany, Spain, Switzerland, and Mexico. He adds that hard times in the economy probably won't have much effect on the company, which he declares "relatively immune" to recessions (perhaps for roughly the same reason that heroin dealers don't sweat what the Fed's doing with interest rates).

And he lets on about another key element in the company's plans—the new Starbucks card, a wallet-size piece of paid-up-front plastic that's "refillable" as necessary. He doesn't come right out and say that the card is ultimately intended to replace all local currencies or serve as mandatory identification when the planetary takeover comes— but that would be giving too much away, wouldn't it? The card, he says, "increases customer loyalty and is a platform on which we'll build." (Ah, but build *what?*)

Then—surprise!—it's time for a third video. This one purports to show how customers love their Starbucks cards. One Generation X'er admits that if he had actual money in his pocket, he would just blow it on *things*. This way he's got forty dollars for a latté. Cool.

After that, Smith introduces DoubleShot, a canned drink consisting of two shots of espresso and one of cream. "It's guaranteed to get you going," he says, laughing nervously at the double entendre. The stuff is supposed to go on sale two months later, but that afternoon I discover cases of DoubleShot on the shelves of a Rite Aid store just down the street. (Local residents often get an early peek at new Starbucks products, because the company uses Seattle as a test market.)

That's followed by an international summary consisting almost entirely of explaining who Starbucks' business partners are in each country. There's no distinguishable pattern to the international arrangements. In the Middle East, Starbucks is in bed with a real estate giant. In Spain it consorts with the company that started a huge Mexican retail store chain. And in Mexico the plan is to link up with the world's largest Domino's pizza franchise.

Smith piggybacks on the discussion of places that aren't the United States by introducing the fourth video of the day. It features happy coffee pickers and describes the company's efforts to bring education to the growers' families.

Yes, that's all swell. But what has Starbucks done here at home? Video number five answers that question with a look at warm-and-fuzzy stuff the company and its employees have been doing in the United States. It concludes with the cloying, overdirected voice of a child predictably squeaking, "Thanks, Starbucks."

Smith appears again to introduce a company rep who works with the bean growers, and for a second it looks like she may tell us what it's like in such exotic foreign lands as Colombia, Brazil, and maybe even Hawaii. But no. She's up there just long enough to say, "People in source countries often say, 'Mary, you do so much in our country. Why do you never talk about it?'" Perhaps because she doesn't need to: Her two sentences are the perfectly flimsy intro for a video describing how Starbucks is benefiting farmers. It is video number *six*. I'm starting to hanker for popcorn.

Smith returns to discuss how the company reacted to the September 11 attacks, the subject of yet *another* brief video. He tells a gripping tale of a man who had escaped from the fifty-fifth floor of the World Trade Center's North Tower and was five blocks from the scene, blinded by a cloud of smoke and dust, when he was pulled to relative safety by someone wearing a green apron. It was, needless to say, a Starbucks employee.

Both of these people are present, of course, and Smith has them stand to receive the crowd's applause. Then he notes that Starbucks employees actually slept in the stores near Ground Zero in the weeks following the attack, to keep the doors open all night long, and that one outlet was still keeping those hours. It's uplifting stuff, appropriately followed by a return of the gospel choir with an energetic but seemingly endless version of "We Believe We Can Fly."

Finally, Schultz is back at center stage to handle the portion of the meeting when shareholders can offer proposals (if they've met a plethora of filing requirements). Evidently one of the company's PR minders has had a quick chat with Schultz, because this time he's toting a Starbucks mug.

It's not easy to get proposals onto meeting agendas. Submissions must be made many months in advance and can be tossed out if the Securities and Exchange Commission says so. (The rules are spelled out at length on the SEC's Web site—www.sec.gov. In the "Fast Answers" section, click on "Proxy Statements, Shareholder Proposals.")

Shareholder proposals rarely get many "for" votes. The largest shareholders in big companies like Starbucks are almost invariably institutional money managers—mutual funds, pension funds, and their ilk—and they tend to vote however the company's managers recommend. That's not surprising. After all, it's likely that they invest in the company because they like how the executives think.

Sponsors of shareholder proposals are typically pension funds (the largest is the California Public Employees' Retirement System, representing the pension interests of more than 1.4 million Californians), nonprofit groups, or individuals with a pet cause. Ironically, to make a proposal, a shareholder must invest a minimum of two thousand dollars in the very company he or she is criticizing, or represent someone else who has invested at least that much. The results of votes on shareholder proposals are typically binding only if a corporation's bylaws say they are, and you can imagine how often that's the case (18 out of 1,056 in 2005, according to Institutional Shareholder Services, which offers voting advice to big money managers who feel they're too busy to study the issues themselves). Indeed, a friend of mine says that shareholder proposals are roughly equivalent to "shouting at the ump."

So in many cases the point of making a proposal is to pressure the company to reconsider its ways and/or to generate press attention. A popular tactic is to offer comments at one year's meeting and follow up with a formal proposal the next year only if the company hasn't addressed the issue. At PetSmart's 2005 shareholder meeting in Boston, a young woman from People for the Ethical Treatment of Animals read a statement suggesting that the company shouldn't sell certain birds. Later she told me that the main reason for her visit was to get a dialogue started and "to let them know that I'm a person from PETA and I don't have three heads."

Schultz seems to have little tolerance for shareholder proposals. He announces that each presenter will be limited to five minutes, introduces the presenters with undisguised disdain, then stares at them, fidgeting and licking his lips while they make their cases. (Five minutes is somewhat generous, actually. Three minutes is more typical. Companies aren't required to provide any presentation time at all, although it's a common courtesy. In 2006 Whole Foods just said no.)

A representative of a nonprofit group called As You Sow—which identifies itself as "dedicated to ensuring that corporations act responsibly and in the long-term best interests of the environment and the human condition"— stands and offers a proposal that would require Starbucks to identify and label genetically modified ingredients in products it sells. He speaks softly and perhaps a bit too politely, wasting valuable time acknowledging that the company has already made efforts to avoid using genetically modified milk. Of course, even an outstanding presentation isn't likely to mean much, because most votes on shareholder proposals (and everything else) have already been cast before the meeting.

Schultz is watching the clock and interrupts in mid-sentence, saying, "I believe your five minutes is up." The presenter asks for an additional thirty seconds. Schultz repeats more firmly, "I believe your five minutes is *up*," and the presenter's microphone goes dead. It's reminiscent of the kangaroo court scene in *Animal House*, where Dean Wormer cuts short the Delta frat boys' defense by shouting "Not another word!"

I'm surprised at this exchange, given Starbucks' reputation for being socially progressive. It's easy to understand how executives might not care for shareholder proposals, though. When you run a business day to day, it's probably irritating to have an absentee owner turn up with different ideas about how you should do things.

But there's plenty of warning about shareholder proposals. Question-and-answer sessions, on the other hand, can be far more treacherous territory. Not here, though. After taking a few softball questions about various products, Schultz wraps up—noting that the shareholder proposals failed—and we're headed for the exits. The giveaways are generous: ice cream bars plus goodie bags filled with coffee beans, cans of DoubleShot, and Starbucks cards loaded to the tune of $3.50. Most shareholders, as they reach the sidewalk, are so busy exploring the goodie bags that they barely notice the protesters handing out flyers warning of unnatural activities by a monster called Frankenbucks.

Wandering around town that afternoon, I resist countless opportunities to use the Starbucks card I've just received. The next morning, waiting for my plane at Sea-Tac Airport, I finally succumb—or at least I try to. But the person behind the counter at the kiosk looks at the shiny new card and says it can't be used in airport locations yet.

Odds are it can't be used where I'm headed next, either.

In a nutshell . . .

STARBUCKS

EDUCATIONAL VALUE: **D**
   Misplacing Hawaii angers the grading god.
ENTERTAINMENT VALUE: **B**
   Eight videos, band, choir.
FREEBIES: **A**
   Product samples, preloaded Starbucks cards.
FOOD & DRINK: **A**
   Terrific breakfast buffet—and lots of coffee.

INSIGHT: Companies don't have to get everything right to be hugely successful. Despite going to great lengths to prepare a seamless show—including lots of videos and a band from South America—Starbucks isn't perfect. When a company actively encourages shareholders to attend the annual meeting, it runs the risk of letting the owners see flaws. But much is forgiven when a company dominates its category, sells a product many people say they can't live without, and truly does get most things right.

3

Mild Thing
OTTER TAIL

Disclosure: During the dot-com years, I yearned for boring utilities with predictable dividends. Otter Tail, which keeps the lights on in part of Minnesota and the Dakotas, appealed to my no-nukes sensibilities. It didn't hurt that Bill Gates, who is known to be a pretty bright guy, owns a chunk of the company.

Time to think small. After seeing how Berkshire Hathaway and Starbucks did things at their shareholder gatherings, I want an example of a lesser-known company. Otter Tail seems like a good bet. After all, how many shareholders would turn up for the annual meeting of a prairie utility an hour outside Fargo? You'd be surprised. More than five hundred people opt to spend the better part of a chilly Monday in the conference area at the local Best Western, catching up on Otter Tail. The company is a favorite investment for the locals. It has served them well over the years, paying an ever-increasing dividend. And once a year it buys them lunch and puts on a show.

To be in Fergus Falls, Minnesota, you have to really want to be in Fergus Falls, Minnesota. It's not on the way to much of anything. That may well be part of its attraction for those who call the city home. Truth is, people aren't exactly moving to the area in droves. The populations of Minnesota and South Dakota are growing more slowly than the national average, while North Dakota's has been shrinking. Recognizing the trend, the folks who run Otter Tail started diversifying more than two decades ago. These days Otter Tail is a mini-conglomerate also including a diagnostic imaging firm, a trucking outfit, a boat supplies manufacturer, and a host of other relatively small companies that seem to play well together. Most, but not all, are based in the area.

I've long had a fondness for this part of the world and an admiration for the people who live here. Anyone who survives the winters is bound to be a hardy and resourceful soul. When I arrive on a Friday night in early April, there's still plenty of snow on the ground and an arctic wind is blowing. Although the Best Western is just off the interstate, I somehow get turned around and end up driving down the three-block main street of Fergus Falls. It's charming—more than a bit reminiscent of Bedford Falls, Jimmy Stewart's hometown in *It's a Wonderful Life*. Little white fairy lights are everywhere, the storefronts are immaculate, and the sidewalks are clean. But no one seems to be around, and when I finally reach the Best Western, the marquee indicates I've just missed some sort of bison ranchers' get-together.

I have pretty much the entire weekend to explore Fergus Falls, arguably more time than is needed in a town where the most prominent tourist attraction is "The World's Largest Otter"—a thirty-foot-long, twelve-foot-high sculpture typical of Minnesota's weird and wonderful monuments. (Among similar attention-getters elsewhere in the state are the "World's Largest" Mallard, Turkey, Cod, Lumberjack, Ox Cart, Ball of Twine, and Hockey Stick.) And it doesn't take long to find Fergus Falls' namesake. It's near the center of town, just across from Otter Tail's headquarters. Niagara has nothing to fear. In fact, the indoor pool at the hotel is a far more impressive water feature—huge, and shaped exactly like the state of Minnesota! Colorado or Kansas, sure. But Minnesota's borders do more than a bit of zigging and zagging.

The hotel bar, Hero's, is the area hotspot on weekend nights, and it's jammed when I duck in. There's a pretty good cover band doing justice to Bob Seger's "Turn the Page." Beers are cheap and cold. Cigarette smoke and alcohol-induced bravado are thick in the air. I overhear two cowboys talking about a third: "That guy won't find his way back to Fargo tonight," draws in response, "Hey, that guy won't even find his truck tonight."

On Monday morning I wander over to the Bigwood Event Center for the Otter Tail gathering. It's not much of a wander, because the center—named for former Otter Tail CEO and chairman Bob Bigwood—is located just across the lobby of the hotel. I'm stunned by how many fellow shareholders are mingling by the registration table. Many are elderly, and most are wearing their Sunday best.

Why on earth are all these people *here*? It's not like they're going to get to spend the day learning from Warren Buffett or drinking enough free high-octane joe to stay up all week.

The souvenirs aren't a big draw, either. There are stacks of Otter Tail pins, Otter Tail pens, and Otter Tail pocket date books. It's the corporate equivalent of giving apples to trick-or-treaters because you happened to have some on hand and didn't happen to have any candy. Of course, when a company's main product is electricity, it's tough to hand out samples.

I'm still puzzling over the turnout when I find myself talking with Bruce Thom, a big man wearing a badge that identifies him as a senior vice president of Otter Tail. Rather than ask the question that's really on my mind—why are all these people here?—I inquire about the Fargo-Moorhead Redhawks, the Northern League baseball team that's Otter Tail's quirkiest subsidiary. He laughs and explains that the company inherited the team when it bought an area radio station. When it subsequently sold the broadcast operation, the team wasn't part of the deal. "It's been good public relations and we've actually made money," he tells me.

Inside the meeting room, I finally understand how Otter Tail has drawn such a crowd—a free lunch! Think high-school lunchroom, with rows of tables running the length of the room. On the tables are water glasses, silverware, and napkins. Chairs face each other across the tables, inviting more conversation among shareholders than there would be at a meeting where everyone was in chairs facing the same direction.

Several of my tablemates are Otter Tail retirees. One, a lady who has lived in Fergus Falls all her life, says the town is known for three things: "geese, police, and old people." I'm chuckling at that when a waitress provides the ultimate icebreaker. Hurrying to fill water glasses before the meeting begins, she trips and spills more than a little very . . . very . . . very . . . *cold* water right down my back, drenching my jacket and pants. Everyone offers napkins to mop up the mess as I exact promises that no one will give me any grief about the wet pants later on.

The chill is fading when John Erickson, Otter Tail's

president, stands, way across the room, and gets the company's 2002 annual meeting (its ninety-third) under way. Right away, it's a down-home affair: He asks if the people who had come more than five hundred miles for the meeting would stand up. Only about twenty of us do, and his subsequent remarks indicate that most everyone else is an Otter Tail employee, an Otter Tail retiree, or an Otter Tail customer—and that this gathering is a town meeting for the good folks of Fergus Falls.

So I'm surrounded by investors who deal with Otter Tail firsthand every day. That's a pretty good way for people to know what they own. Of course, if you only invest in companies whose products or services are a regular part of your life, you'll miss out on those that don't do business where you live—a lot of utilities and banks, for starters. Sometimes those opportunities can be among the very best, because they're off Wall Street's radar, too.

Erickson quickly describes how the company has been diversifying by buying small businesses and continuing to operate them as stand-alone companies or by rolling them into existing operations. He says Otter Tail is decentralized; in other words, the parent company generally keeps its nose out of things.

There's talk about the company's various subsidiaries and a brief presentation by representatives of one. DMI originally made sugar beet processing equipment. When the beet processing industry collapsed in the late 1990s, DMI's employees asked themselves what they were really good at and decided it was "building and shaping big metal things." So DMI reinvented itself as a maker of windmills—the big kind, with towers up to 250 feet tall and 14 1/2 inches around. This part of the country is an especially promising area for wind power. Neighboring

North Dakota, we're told, has the potential to produce enough energy by harnessing the wind to satisfy one third of the power needs of the continental United States.

I think this is inspiring and fascinating stuff, but it's lost on the snoring retiree seated next to me. He's enjoying a Zen experience—a comfortable chair and soothing reassurances that Otter Tail's being run exactly like you would expect a utility in a small town in the Midwest to be run: prudently. The dividend is up. Receivables are in good shape. The ratings agencies think highly of Otter Tail. And there's none of that "pro forma" mumbo-jumbo in the company's earnings statements.

Suddenly it's time for the main event: lunch. I had figured that company executives might answer questions during the meal; I figured wrong. Just before our waitress gets another crack at me, word comes from the lectern that any questions submitted in writing "will be answered by the company in due course"—but not at the meeting itself!

If this were a big-city company, I would raise an eyebrow. Maybe both. But I've spent enough time in this part of the world over the years to appreciate that Midwesterners tend to mean what they say, and for that reason I favor stocks of companies located anywhere between, say, Albany and Sacramento. It's more than a coincidence, I think, that Warren Buffett hails from and continues to live in Omaha. (Incidentally, although a Q&A session is customary at shareholder meetings, it's not required. Target skipped the custom altogether in 2003. Home Depot did the same in 2006, angering shareholders with questions about why the CEO's pay rose while the stock price fell.)

As salads begin to appear on tables, an earnest lounge singer belts out a few songs. When plates filled with pork

roasts, potatoes, and carrots come along, he's replaced by
two manic comediennes who call themselves Tina and
Leena. Their specialty is "Olie and Leena" material—
slightly off-color jokes based on innocent-but-clueless
Scandinavian characters quite recognizable to most residents of Min-uh-so-da. But the irrepressible duo veers off
in other directions, too—leading the crowd through
rousing versions of "I Saw the Light" and "Roll Out the
Barrel" before pointing out an unsuspecting white-haired
shareholder and introducing her as "former first lady Barbara Bush!" The crowd eats it up.

I don't find the lunch very appealing, but the crowd
eats that up, too. Perhaps the fact that it was free has
something to do with it, but I think it's more about the
camaraderie—their friends, their neighbors, their town,
their company.

True, there's no six-hour Q&A—and there's no Starbucks in this town or the next one or the next one—but
I'm going to sit right here and savor this experience. At
least until my pants dry.

In a nutshell . . .

OTTER TAIL

EDUCATIONAL VALUE: **B**
    In-depth look at one subsidiary's business.
ENTERTAINMENT VALUE: **B**
    Singer, comediennes.
FREEBIES: **C**
    Date books, pens.
FOOD & DRINK: **B**
    It's not gourmet cuisine, but it's lunch.

INSIGHT: "Buy what you know" works well if you want to limit yourself to companies that make products or services easily available to you. What if you want to invest in companies that don't serve your area? Many regional utilities and banks are solid businesses with long histories of rewarding shareholders. Sometimes they offer the added advantage of being relatively unknown on Wall Street, so Joe and Jane Customer may know as much or more about the company as anyone in the investment business. Attending the shareholder meeting of a regional company allows you to hear what the company and its customers (often the largest part of the shareholder base for a regional company) have to say. If the company is the town's major employer—as Otter Tail is in tiny Fergus Falls—it's not unusual for the person next to you to be a shareholder of the company, a customer of the company, and a retired (or current) employee of the company.

4

The Great American Chocolate Spar

HERSHEY

Disclosure: When I was a kid, I broke out in a rash if I ate dark choco-late. So every Easter my mother found me a white chocolate bunny—tasty, but not really chocolate at all. Fortunately, I outgrew this allergy! My taste in chocolates these days runs more toward See's—indeed, if I come home empty-handed from a trip to a city where there's a See's store, my wife will probably change the locks. But when I first started seriously evaluating stocks—trying to figure out whether the share price was genuinely attractive, and why—Hershey looked especially sweet. With its long record of paying dividends, I figured it was a stock I would buy and hold forever.

There's a giant rat outside the door. It's an inflatable rodent, true, but not the sort of thing you want to associate with a candy company. That's precisely why Chocolate Workers Local #464 has brought it to the Hershey Theater on this gloomy afternoon in spring 2002. The union—which represents twenty-seven hundred employees currently on strike in this company town where the streetlights are shaped like Hershey's Kisses—wants everyone to know that it thinks Hershey's chairman/presi-dent/CEO, Richard Lenny, is one unsavory creature.

A few days earlier the workers walked out because the company said it would require employees to pay more for health care. Now they're gathered, with picket signs, almost anywhere that shareholders in town for today's meeting might venture. The workers obviously feel that Lenny's cost-cutting efforts are at odds with his paycheck.

Strikes are rare at Hershey. This is only the fifth since the company was founded in 1894, and the first in more than two decades. Indeed, the company has long been renowned for its generosity to employees and local residents. Founder Milton Hershey poured much of the company's profits back into the community. The town that took the company name boasts any number of facilities paid for by the candy maker, including an ice rink, a hotel, an amusement park (Hersheypark), and the Hershey Theater itself. There's also the founder's pride and joy: a school for disadvantaged children. Long before he died in 1945, Milton Hershey gave much of his own money to the school. These days the school is supported by dividend income from the Hershey Trust, which owns more than two-thirds of the company's shares.

Unfortunately, Hershey's stock price has gone stagnant in recent years. So the board decided to shake things up by bringing in an outsider—the highly polished fifty-year-old Lenny, who had made his mark at Nabisco. The move has had the desired effect, sweetening the share price over the short haul, but perhaps at the cost of threatening a century of congeniality.

Before the meeting, shareholders received a letter acknowledging as much by warning that security would be extraordinary. It's not unusual, of course, for companies to ask shareholders to bring copies of their statements.

Hershey made that worth the trouble by offering a tasty reward—a box filled with packages of Reese's Pieces, Hershey's Kisses, Jolly Rancher lollipops, Ice Breakers mints, and Hershey's Milk Chocolate with Almond Bites, plus a couple of namesake candy bars and a new one called Fast Break. The giveaways were distributed at the relatively tranquil reception area for Chocolate World, the corporate visitor's center, which is next to the amusement park, a few miles away from the meeting location.

Here at Hershey Theater, there's a traffic jam at the entrance. We shareholders first have to navigate our way through a crowd of protesters who are shouting and handing out leaflets. Meanwhile, the line for the two metal detectors just inside the door is moving at a snail's pace, and it comes to a halt for a few minutes when the guy in front of me turns out to be carrying a tiny penknife. Even by post–September 11 standards, it's clear that the guards are taking no chances with the crowd. The only attendees exempted from careful scrutiny are a few very elderly folks.

The registration tables are overwhelmed. By the time I'm signed in, they're saying that the main theater is filled and shuffling attendees toward another room—the Hershey Miniature Theater, at the other end of the building. It's linked by video with the main meeting room and seems to be populated largely by agitated union representatives who are also shareholders.

When I find a seat, Lenny's already onscreen offering gee-whiz facts about the company. He says Hershey sells 43 percent of all the chocolate in the country and 31 percent of all the candy. He adds that the company's market share exceeds that of rivals Mars, Nestlé, and Wrigley, combined. He observes that Hershey has eleven different brands with annual sales of more than $100 million.

The union folks around me can't find anything to object to in those introductory remarks, and they shift nervously in their seats as Lenny talks about the company's past, present, and future. He says prospects are good, citing research: 30 percent of all daily calories ingested by Americans now come from snacks, and half of all candy is purchased on impulse. Those figures are scary for anyone worried about the country's collective waistline, but they seem to sound pretty good to most Hershey shareholders.

Then, for the first time today, Lenny tries to reach out to the employees. He probably doesn't intend for his remark that he's "proudest of the loyal and dedicated workforce" to get a laugh, but it gets a big one.

Lenny quickly retreats to business school jargon that leaves a lot of us in the audience scratching our heads. Within a few short minutes, he works all of these buzzwords and phrases into his patter: *optimizing . . . value-added . . . results-driven . . . rationalize . . . streamline asset base . . . SKU rationalization . . . EDC3 . . . scale leverage . . . brand-building . . . selling initiatives . . . performance barriers . . . synergistically.* (I look at the list later and find I can make some sense of most of them. But "EDC3?")

He tells us that during the past year, Hershey has sold or closed several facilities, cut staff, and reduced inventory. The company has brought new blood into headquarters, where nine of the ten top executives took on their roles during the past eighteen months. And the product pipeline is filled with such delicacies as Mini-Reese's Easter eggs and "special edition" dark chocolate Kisses.

Lenny says the efforts have been reflected in Hershey's stock price, which has been rising even as the market as a whole has been moving in the other direction. Then he

takes another crack at mending the rift with employees:
"What's most gratifying is that our people have embraced
the changes." I hear snickering around me. (Er, maybe
that was mere laughter. Snickers are made by Hershey's
rival, Mars.)

Suddenly we're off to the movies. The words "Great
people, great brands" appear on the screen for a few seconds, then there's a series of propaganda clips featuring
smiling employees saying phrases like "a great place to
work" and "committed to its people." The final clip features an enthusiastic employee saying, "We're going to
places nobody ever thought we would." Music swells, and
within seconds that prophesy comes true. The Q&A portion of the meeting is nothing less than a public meltdown.

First to the microphone is a union rep who observes
that the video presentation didn't include a single
employee from the local that's now on strike. Then he
brings the house down by asking Lenny what the union
feels is the multimillion-dollar question: "Why can't we
just take a small portion of what you're paid and settle this
contract?" The crowd roars.

Lenny waits for the noise to die down, then calmly
responds that his salary for the past year was $600,000,
with a bonus of $900,000 and $3.2 million in restricted
shares (which he can't sell without special permission).
There are also some stock options that vest over four
years. In any case, Lenny says, pay levels are set by the
board of directors, so he focuses on other concerns.

Then he gets a bit too defensive: "I'm here to do what
the shareholders want me to do, which is to increase
shareholder value." It reminds me of when a politician
invokes what he or she claims are the feelings of "the
American people." Nobody in this audience is interested

in *decreasing* shareholder value, but interpretations vary. Some investors may want quick gains while others want consistent growth. Lenny seems to be talking to the former, not the latter.

Then one of the most disturbing incidents I've ever seen at a shareholder meeting takes place.

It's not unusual for parents to push nervous kids or grandkids toward a microphone during the Q&A portion of a shareholder meeting. It happens all the time at Berkshire Hathaway meetings, for example. I'm sure the adults mean well and figure the tykes will appreciate, later in life, that they can say they once talked with Warren Buffett. Too often, the kids stumble through a script clearly written by a stage-managing adult. It's like watching kids who are being forced to learn to play the piano just because their parents never did.

But today the practice hits a new low when a boy who looks to be about eight approaches the mike and says, "I am a stockholder and I want to know why the strikers are so mad."

Mind you, that's what he *says*. What everyone *hears* is "I'm a cute kid and it wouldn't look good if you didn't take me seriously. Mr. CEO, when did you stop beating your wife?" For a few seconds, the air is sucked out of the room.

Lenny, to his credit, treats the question as though it had been asked by an adult (as it almost certainly was, indirectly). He uses phrases that probably wouldn't mean much to the kid but does his best to spell out the issues and his hope for resolution. It's a strong performance, and it seems to take some of the steam out of the union members, if only temporarily.

A senior union guy stands and rambles on incoherently for quite awhile about some perceived injustice related to where he was seated for the meeting (in the annex, where I am). Finally it's clear he isn't even going to ask an actual question, so he sits down.

He's not the only elderly attendee whose train of thought may have run off the tracks. A woman who identifies herself as a Hershey retiree lodges some sort of complaint about Hershey product labels showing what she believes are incorrect locations of factories before suggesting that the company should try combining maple syrup with chocolate. Apparently she tried it and "it tasted real nice."

By now the union has regrouped and is ready to have another go at Lenny's throat. The business agent for Local #464 says that Hershey's retirees were apparently recognized at a recent dinner as "the greatest asset to the company"— just days before they got word that their medical benefits were to be cut. (The "greatest asset" bit is a noble sentiment, but benefits for retirees are, after all, liabilities.)

A woman stands and gets in a sneaky jab with what sounds, at first, like praise. She tells Lenny she wants to compliment him: "I understand you recently met with retirees to teach them how to manage their *fixed income*." The line gets the second-biggest laugh of the day from the union crowd.

Another woman, who says she's been at Hershey for thirty-one years, asks why employees at the local plants are being asked to pay more for health care. A company spokesman explains that 60 percent of all Hershey employees already contribute 10 percent for their own health care. The employees on strike, he says, currently contribute only 6 percent, and the notion behind the new plan is to get all employees in sync.

That doesn't wash for some in the crowd. They aren't as worried about disparities between their paychecks and those of their colleagues as they are about disparities between their paychecks and those of the people *onstage*. One very nervous late-shift worker says, "You're spending a lot of money against us—more than you would have paid us." Looking at Lenny, he continues, "Your salary is $852 an hour. It's time to share."

Lenny seems to show a trace of anger at last. "I didn't come here for the money," he responds in a measured tone, adding that he feels he earned last year's pay.

The next few questions are less controversial and help to cool tensions somewhat.

A diabetic chocolate lover asks if there are any sugar-free products in the works. Lenny smiles and says he understands this question has come up year after year, then vows to introduce sugar-free products soon.

Another shareholder, noting that two Hershey board members are executives at Lincoln National Life but knowing nothing about the long-established and well-respected Indiana insurance company, asks, "That company's not like that *Enron*, are they?" Lenny laughs and says, "No. They're like us. They're a real company and they make real money." Many in the crowd laugh with him, and for a moment it seems possible that the dark cloud over the meeting may have lifted.

It hasn't. Another obviously coached kid comes to the microphone and asks, "If the strike goes long, how will you deal with it?" Lenny doesn't really answer but assures the boy, "We all want to get this behind us."

There's time for just one more question, but the final shareholder to speak doesn't have one. Instead he uses the opportunity to simply wonder aloud whatever happened to the spirit of Milton Hershey, who focused on treating employees with respect while building the nation's number one chocolate company.

It's a poignant thought for shareholders leaving the meeting to consider, and surely not what Hershey executives would have preferred as a finale.

Outside, it's raining. The huge inflatable rat is gone and so are many of the picketers. I walk briskly to my car and spend the next few hours on the highway doing some quality control testing on the candy samples I had received earlier. For years I've been hearing that chocolate tickles the happy cells in our brains. After the past few hours I may need to eat the whole box.

In a nutshell . . .

HERSHEY

EDUCATIONAL VALUE: **B**
Learned a lot about union/management politics.

ENTERTAINMENT VALUE: **B**
Would've made a good reality TV episode.

FREEBIES: **A**
Sampler box of Hershey products.

FOOD & DRINK: **D**
Free coffee. Big deal.

INSIGHT: If the employees aren't happy, there's trouble at the company—and you, as an owner, should know about it. Confrontations at shareholder meetings can put both sides of an argument in perspective and provide a sense of how far away resolution might be. Of course, it's important to remember that participants are keenly aware they're onstage. Some shine in the spotlight, others are hams, and some are just plain bad actors.

5

Good Golly Miss Gadfly

GANNETT

*Disclosure: Somewhere around age seven, I got the bright idea to pro-
duce a newspaper for my neighborhood outside Rochester, New York.
So I put pencil to paper and created my first issue. When I realized
that I might need additional copies, I made two or three more by hand.
Then I went around the block and sold out my "press run" for a penny
a copy—an early indication that I needed to work on my business sense.
Gannett, which published Rochester's morning and evening newspapers, never felt the competition. Over the years, the company has
become the dominant newspaper publisher in many mid-sized U.S.
cities like Rochester. In 1982 it introduced* USA Today, *the ubiquitous "McPaper." In late 2000—before most people started turning to
the Internet for news—I bought shares in Gannett.*

"I'm not done yet!" shouts Evelyn Davis, a slight but
fierce woman in her seventies, before she continues
rambling in her thick Dutch accent about how any
number of things that offend her are *"outrageous!"* Gannett's CEO/chairman/president, Doug McCorkindale,
gives up and lets her keep talking. The digital clock projected on the screen at the front of the room—the one he
has already noted is there to help confine Davis's remarks
to three minutes—starts showing numbers in red.

Davis is unquestionably the queen of corporate gad-flies. She owns shares in nearly a hundred companies and visits dozens of shareholder meetings each year to taunt executives and tout herself. In her spare time Davis writes, edits, and publishes *Highlights and Lowlights*, a newsletter aimed exclusively at CEOs who are willing to shell out more than a thousand dollars a year to subscribe and per-haps stay on her good side.

Executives certainly don't want to draw her scorn, because she's been known to say just about anything at a shareholder meeting. Several veteran observers have shared with me the tale of when she famously told former Citigroup CEO John Reed, "I've got you by the balls!"

Among Davis's pet peeves are staggered elections for board seats. When only a minority of directors are up for reelection each year, revolution is impossible.

That was one of many issues first raised by pioneer cor-porate gadflies, Lewis and John Gilbert. The brothers—who, with the rest of their family, owned a small number of shares in about six hundred companies—started speaking up at shareholder meetings in the 1930s, when such things simply weren't done. As Lewis Gilbert wrote in his book *Dividends and Democracy*, "In 1932, the typical annual meeting, often tucked away in some remote rural hideaway, was usually attended by no more than a silent dispirited baker's dozen who listlessly listened to the mechanical legal jargon by which insiders re-elected themselves to do as they pleased." (Three-quarters of a century later, it's still entirely possible to find meetings matching this description!)

As the owner of ten shares in Consolidated Gas Com-pany, Lewis Gilbert went to the company's annual meeting in February 1932 and tried to ask a question but was ignored by the chairman. When he attended other company meetings over the next few years, chairmen often tried to belittle him by mocking the small number of shares he owned or asking for proof that he owned any at all.

With help from a small group of colleagues (including Wilma Soss, president of the Federation of Women Shareholders), the Gilberts set out on a lifelong crusade to make shareholders' voices count. Often they were able to speak on behalf of other small investors who gave their proxies. (By the way, when you send in your ballot, what you're really doing is giving the directors your proxy to vote your shares as you've indicated—or however they choose, if you haven't indicated. Shareholders haven't always had the freedom to skip the annual meeting itself. Seventeenth-century English joint-stock companies—predecessors of today's corporations— apparently *required* investors to attend and even fined those who didn't show up!)

The Gilberts' demands were similar, in many cases, to those made even today by shareholder activists. They insisted, for example, that dividends for shareholders should take precedence over fat paychecks and stock option grants for executives. Lewis Gilbert believed CEO salaries should be capped at $200,000—and at Bethlehem Steel's 1938 shareholder meeting he proposed eliminating company chairman Charles W. Schwab's $250,000 salary (the equivalent of more than $3 million today).

And pity the directors who didn't own shares in the companies on whose boards they served. At Remington Rand's 1953 shareholder meeting, Lewis Gilbert chastised then-chairman General Douglas MacArthur for not purchasing a stake in the very company he led. By the next year's meeting, MacArthur had waved the white flag and bought some shares.

From 1939 until well into the 1950s, the brothers produced an annual report on annual meetings, rating the chairman at each company. In 1954 the publication was more than two hundred pages long!

We can thank the Gilberts and their gang for quite a few things, including confidentiality of ballots cast by shareholders. Perhaps their most important achievement, though, was getting the Securities and Exchange Commission to file suit against Transamerica, prohibiting the banking giant from holding its meeting until three Gilbert proposals were published in the proxy statement. Two of the proposals called for changing the company's bylaws to guarantee balloting on shareholder proposals at the meeting itself and to allow shareholders to elect the company's auditors. The other sought to require Transamerica to issue a post-meeting report to all shareholders.

Transamerica fought back, saying its existing bylaws permitted the company's board to exclude proposals from the proxy statement. In 1947 Judge John J. Biggs of the Third United States Circuit Court ruled that Transamerica had to comply, observing, "A corporation is run for the benefit of its stockholders and not for that of its managers." As various corporate scandals have proven in recent years, some executives still haven't embraced the judge's opinion.

These days shareholder proposals are relatively common, and most annual meetings include a shareholder vote on the company's outside auditor—although there's never more than one candidate offered. As for post-meeting reports, companies typically opt to include a summary on their Web sites (check the Investor Relations section) or in the next year's first-quarter report. Some produce transcripts and post those or send copies to shareholders. A few, such as Occidental Petroleum, publish a brochure about the meeting and send it to investors who have shown interest in the company.

In addition to opening the doors for shareholders to make and vote on proposals at annual meetings, the Gilberts often brought humor to the gatherings, which had historically consisted of little more than a formal recitation of the financial statements. John, for instance, took to wearing red noses to shareholder meetings after a company chairman called him a clown.

Both brothers lived to see a lot of things change and a lot of things stay the same. Lewis died in 1993 and John passed away in 2002.

They blazed the trail for all the gadflies who have appeared at shareholder meetings to tilt at corporate windmills. For many years the focus was on financial accountability to investors. That began to change in 1967, when radical Saul Alinsky hit on the idea of asking Eastman Kodak's shareholders to demonstrate their unhappiness with the company's minority hiring practices by assigning their proxies to his organization or planning to vote against Kodak on routine matters. The tactic led to a prolonged discussion at Kodak's shareholder meeting, and the company agreed to take positive steps.

Not long after that, opponents of napalm began pushing Dow Chemical to allow shareholders to vote on whether the company should continue to manufacture the deadly defoliant. Dow didn't feel it had to include a shareholder proposal along those lines in its proxy statement, because proposals could not, under existing law, address ordinary business operations, nor could they be made primarily for political or social reasons. The Securities and Exchange

Commission agreed. In mid-1970, though, the decision was overturned by the U.S. Circuit Court of Appeals for the District of Columbia.

Meanwhile, a group of young lawyers put together a nonprofit organization called Project on Corporate Responsibility and—with help from consumer advocate Ralph Nader—chose General Motors as a symbolic target for a flurry of nine proposals related to product safety, pollution control, and employment minority hiring. Like Dow, GM wanted to exclude the proposals from the proxy statement. But the SEC decided two of the proposals had to be included—one to add public representatives to the board of directors and the other to create a shareholder committee on corporate responsibility. Neither got more than 3 percent favorable votes, the threshold required to qualify for reintroduction the next year. Yet the campaign helped draw a great deal of attention to the potential uses of shareholder proposals.

With the advent of the "Greed Is Good" era on Wall Street in the mid-1980s, activists turned their attention to making sure executives weren't the only ones to benefit if an offer was made to buy the company. At Santa Fe's 1988 annual meeting, Robert Monks, founder of Institutional Shareholder Services, was behind a shareholder proposal to prevent the company from implementing a "poison pill" defense to a takeover bid.[1] With 61 percent of the

---

1. No cyanide is involved. A "poison pill" strategy discourages takeover attempts by increasing costs for a potential acquirer. In some instances, the target company might give existing shareholders (other than the suitor) preferred stock they can sell at a premium after a takeover. In other cases, existing shareholders might be allowed to increase their holdings at a bargain price not available to the acquirer, or even to buy shares of the acquirer's stock at a discount.

votes cast in favor, this shareholder proposal became the first ever to win a majority. Yet like nearly all votes on shareholder proposals, it was merely advisory.

Monks, who has described himself as "a 6'6" Harvard Phi Beta Kappa rich WASP happily married to Andrew Carnegie II's granddaughter," is hardly an Average Joe investor. Among other things, he has tried unsuccessfully to get himself nominated as a candidate for the board at Sears and Exxon. When rebuffed in the latter effort, he came back with a resolution that would have had the company paying representatives of the three largest institutional shareholders to make proposals at the annual meetings. So money belonging to all the shareholders—including the Average Joes and Janes, who wouldn't get to vote on the representatives—would have been funneled into the coffers of big investors who would then decide what issues were and weren't important. Some of those big investors, of course, might well have hired Institutional Shareholder Services to look out for their interests.

Not everyone who turns up at a lot of shareholder meetings has a beef. One cold November 2005 morning in Chicago for the annual meeting of a tiny traffic safety company called Quixote, I met computer consultant Maury Wexler, who told me he owns shares in twelve hundred companies—wow!—and goes to shareholder meetings to get his picture taken with CEOs. The scrapbook he proudly carried proved he wasn't kidding. At the same gathering I met Martin Glotzer, who seemed to be something of a "good news" gadfly: He had nothing but praise for the company. I ran into him again at Walgreen's shareholder meeting in early 2006. He had only nice things to say about the pharmacy giant, too.

Other frequent attendees are just . . . well . . . *unusual.*
At a shareholder meeting for Tofutti—a tiny New Jersey
company that makes nondairy treats—one of the few
attendees was a long-haired, bearded man in his late for-
ties, wearing shorts and a T-shirt. He was a nonstop talker
with an impressive intellect, but his most noticeable feature was that his fingernails were several inches long.
Either he's emulating Howard Hughes, or the thirty to
forty shareholder meetings he claims to attend each year
keep him too busy for grooming.

Here at Gannett's 2002 meeting, in the company's
McLean, Virginia, headquarters, a seventyish gentlemen
with perpetually raised eyebrows tells us he's from
"Yonkers, New Yawk—population one nine six oh eight
six," and that the last Gannett meeting he attended was in
April 1987. He announces that he has "some valid and
intelligent questions," then launches a series of baffling
but very exacting inquiries about "dis very fine outstanding company." Among other things, he says to
McCorkindale, "The proxy statement says you are over
sixty-two years of age. When the tragic event of September 11 happened when American Airlines flight
number 11 hit Building 2 at the World Trade Center at
8:42 a.m., how did you receive the news?" McCorkindale
responds that he carried on working, which apparently is
the right answer, because Mr. Precision moves on to
another topic.

All the executives up front seem like deer caught in the
headlights. While their own presentations are completely
scripted and about as innocuous as possible, they can't
control the peanut gallery and there are some tough questions. How *are* they going to deal with the fact that people
are increasingly turning to the Internet for their news

fixes? And will the advertisers who have bailed in favor of the competitor from cyberspace ever return?

McCorkindale and his cohorts tell us they've been trying all sorts of ideas to deal with the challenges—creating special sections intended to appeal to Generation X readers, having papers located near one another share circulation services, and even freezing executive salaries.

Apparently, Gannett has decided to try freezing the shareholders, too. The temperature in the room seems like it's been getting chillier and chillier since the meeting began. Why, a skeptical soul might think someone was cranking up the air conditioning to encourage people to leave without asking more questions! Of course, most of us aren't asking any questions. In fact, most of us probably couldn't get a word in if we tried, because the gadflies are so longwinded.

Most gadflies say they represent the public interest, but they sometimes veer into self-interest. Almost by definition, they're wealthy individuals living off investment income, so it's difficult for them to identify with Average Joe or Jane Investor. Indeed, Lewis Gilbert spent considerable energy insisting that shareholder meetings should be held in Manhattan because it would be most convenient—for New Yorkers like himself.

As for Evelyn Davis, several of her rants before the Gannett crowd include conspicuous plugs for her upcoming appearance on CNBC. This is the first time I've ever crossed paths with Davis, but when I see her at other shareholder meetings later in my travels, she behaves pretty much the same way. Nobody seems to know how to shut her up. Turning the room into a penguin paradise is no more effective than the countdown clock.

Making it difficult to get in apparently won't work,

either. The notice Gannett sent shareholders to announce the meeting specified that anyone interested in attending had to submit a written ticket request at least a week in advance. It's a rule that makes sense for a popular meeting like Berkshire Hathaway's, held in a huge arena. But Berkshire makes it easy, providing a card to fill in and return. Gannett requires anyone who is interested to sit down and write a letter saying so, which seems like an extra hoop meant to trip up anyone who doesn't read the fine print (although in fairness the company probably saves shareholders some money by holding the meeting in Gannett's headquarters building, rather than a hotel ballroom). Altria—the company once known as Philip Morris—also requires shareholders to request tickets in advance, which I didn't notice until after the deadline had passed. Embarrassingly, I'd bought shares in the tobacco giant just to have access to the shareholder meeting.

While gadflies have been known to flap their jaws just to hear themselves talk, ordinary individual shareholders aren't as likely to speak up—unless, of course, they fear their entire investment is going down the drain. That's the case at my next stop.

In a nutshell . . .

GANNETT

EDUCATIONAL VALUE: **D**
Lackluster presentations; no *USA Today* graphics!

ENTERTAINMENT VALUE: **B**
Gadflies provided some buzz.

FREEBIES: **B**
Free papers, tour of newsroom.

FOOD & DRINK: **C**
Bagels, fruit, coffee, OJ.

INSIGHT: Meetings can be forums for gadflies who say they're seeking improvements in corporate governance. Gadflies have been around for decades: Lewis and John Gilbert were pioneers in the 1930s when they had the audacity to suggest shareholders should be heard. Evelyn Davis is today's best-known gadfly, turning up each spring at dozens of shareholder meetings. Unfortunately, gadflies often seem to be as interested in tooting their own horns as in looking out for the interests of fellow shareholders.

6

(This Might Be)
The Last Time

V-ONE

Disclosure: If Warren Buffett doesn't understand technology well enough to feel good about buying shares in a tech company, the odds are I don't, either. I never owned shares in V-One, a company that makes Internet security devices enabling users to create private online networks. A friend who was on the company's board invited me to sit in on V-One's shareholder meeting.

When a company doesn't meet certain share price or volume standards, a stock exchange may decide to "delist" it—no longer accepting buy or sell orders. That's often the kiss of death. Companies will do almost anything to avoid it.

V-One, which went public (first sold shares) in 1996, is on the brink in May 2002. Entire days pass when no shares are traded at all. What's more, in its most recently published financial report, V-One's outside auditors warned that the company may not remain "a going concern" much longer. In the past month, two senior executives have left. Those who remain have deferred salary increases.

We're gathered in a nineteenth-century Rockville, Maryland, mansion that's often used for weddings and art shows. Projected on a pulled-down window shade at the front of the room are the words "V-One is a stronger and more focused Company, fully committed to meet the challenges facing us." It's a message that CEO and president Margaret Grayson—a small woman in her mid-fifties, who is struggling to be heard over the din of a lawnmower outside—is trying to underscore when she calls the most recent period "a rebuilding year."

Sports fans cringe when they hear that phrase, and so do the dozen or so shareholders present. They've lost most of their investment and aren't happy about it. One complains that "the stock price has declined 300 percent"—which isn't mathematically possible, but the exaggeration underscores his impatience. He says he's tired of "wild ups and downs" and wants to know why the share price can't be stabilized.

CEO Grayson doesn't deny that V-One has hit an iceberg but says she thinks giving up the ship would be premature. There are new customers, including the U.S. Army, the FBI, and Southwest Airlines. There's potential business from the Department of Homeland Security. And there's still a chance that other government contracts V-One's been counting on for ages will come through—although an Office of Management and Budget study comparing vendors isn't due to be completed for another two or three years. She concedes it's possible that orders are being held back because of questions about V-One's viability.

Grayson adds that she has agreed to serve on the National Infrastructure Advisory Council reporting to President Bush, and she hopes to take full advantage of the opportunity to get some attention for V-One's software.

Meanwhile, Grayson says, the company has been busy

repositioning what she repeatedly calls "the product." It wasn't suited to the small end of the market or the large end, she says, so the notion now is to push it as a "large enterprise solution." I'm probably the only non-techie in the room, but I have no idea what she's talking about. Are large enterprises a problem? (Has Captain Kirk been informed?)

Actually, the problem seems to be one that's plagued a lot of high-tech companies in recent years: The company is going through cash faster than it's earning it. Although Grayson says revenues are up a bit and expenses are down, what's called the "burn rate" in industry parlance isn't looking good.

"How long can things go on like this before the money's all gone?" asks one frustrated shareholder. "Why can't V-One get the word out about what it has to offer?"

With that, chairman of the board William Odom—a burly retired lieutenant general who has been pretty quiet until now—finally blows his top. "We're screaming at the top of our lungs! We're up against some very big companies. I don't know if we'll make it. Our transformation over the past eighteen months has been dramatic, but we should have made cuts three years ago. We don't have the resources to get the word out. We've tried that. We're counting on performance, on word-of-mouth. Whether it's in time to save us, I don't know."

Grayson responds to the same question differently: "The more good news we put out, the more money investors take off the table."

A shareholder seated in front of me shakes her head back and forth to indicate she disagrees. "The stock isn't trading much," she says.

"It's trading enough for people to take advantage of the spread.[1] The good shareholders are being taken advantage of by those who buy our stock because it's a distress situation," Grayson says.

"The solution," she continues, "is to merge or get additional financing. We're in the process of exploring all options." She talks about her hope for a strategic alliance—a partnership with a stronger company. So far, efforts to find such a relationship have failed. Grayson thinks that's because "the product" wasn't ready for prime time, but these days it is.

Molly Bayley, a former vice president at NASDAQ, an experienced financial services consultant, and a member of the company's board for the past two years, is taking it all in. She's one of six directors, but not one of the two up for reelection at this meeting.

Directors don't have to attend shareholder meetings unless it's required by the company's bylaws. In many cases, directors are strongly encouraged to come to the shareholder meeting, which is often scheduled just prior to a board meeting. Home Depot, ExxonMobil, Bank of America, Microsoft, Intel, Motorola, FedEx, Alcoa, and Comcast are among companies without such requirements, but most companies believe it's important for directors to be present so that shareholders can see their elected representatives in the flesh. Another reason— especially for Bayley and other "outside" directors (those

---

1. The spread is the difference between the "bid" price (what a potential purchaser of shares is willing to pay) and the "ask" price (what a potential seller would like to receive) for the shares. If a stock is thinly traded (not many shares change hands each day), the difference between the two figures can be considerable. The spreads on widely held stocks are usually no more than a penny per share.

who aren't otherwise affiliated with the company)—is to be able to listen to questions asked by shareholders and answered by the staff.

It can't be easy for V-One's directors to hear what they're hearing. "If I didn't have confidence in the staff, I'd be worried," Bayley says later. Demonstrating their commitment to the company, she and the other members of the board have waived their fees of one thousand dollars a month for overseeing V-One's management.

Companies don't live forever. Some make a big splash in their lifetimes but are ultimately lost to the ages: American Beet Sugar, International Shoe, and Studebaker were once big enough deals that they were components of the Dow Jones Industrial Average. Others never really get traction. It's a sad thing to see a company die and to see stockholders and stakeholders in various stages of denial and acceptance.

Today I've seen people losing their tempers because they're afraid they're going to lose their shirts. Everyone in the room would rather be someplace else—perhaps on a nice warm island. Fortunately for me, that's where I'm headed next.

In a nutshell . . .

V-One

EDUCATIONAL VALUE: **D**
Hard to follow tech talk.

ENTERTAINMENT VALUE: **C**
Occasionally painful to watch/hear.

FREEBIES: **F**
None.

FOOD & DRINK: **C**
Decent breakfast spread.

INSIGHT: Patient shareholders who have gnashed their teeth for months can use the annual meeting to vent their frustrations. Technology companies are often among the most rewarding investments, but they're also among the riskiest. If things go sour, investors left holding the bag often feel they have a lot to shout about.

No Ukes

HAWAIIAN ELECTRIC

Disclosure: I purchased shares in Hawaiian Electric after noting, on a trip to Maui, that Hawaii's only publicly traded electric utility is truly a business surrounded by the largest of moats. In addition, the company— which also includes American Savings Bank, one of Hawaii's largest banking networks—has been paying dividends since 1901.

I figure that the dress code for shareholder meetings is similar to the dress code for flying on an airplane. There was a time when doing either one called for putting on your very best duds, and even now you'll probably get treated a bit better if you do.

But one of the privileges of owning part of a business is that you can dress however you like for the shareholder meeting. While I've seen jeans and Bermuda shorts, some sort of "business casual" approach usually strikes the right note. On rare occasions I'll don a suit; more often I'll opt for a white shirt, Dockers, and maybe a tan sport coat. It's hard to go far wrong with that combination.

Except here at Hawaiian Electric, where it's clear that I missed a memo. All the employees, from the very top down, are wearing Hawaiian shirts, which turn out to be everyday dress at the company. Because it's shareholder meeting day, they've added name tags lest all those people in garish outfits start to look alike. The other shareholders favor similar togs, so the room is a sea of Day-Glo orange, lime green, and iridescent blue. I'm tempted to keep my sunglasses on.

A reception is being held in a room normally used for training by American Savings Bank, a company subsidiary. It's jammed, and it takes a few minutes to get to the refreshment tables, where I'm pleased to find pineapple cake, bread pudding, doughnuts, coffee, and orange juice. While nibbling, I read the bulletin boards and watch as shareholders chat with company reps.

We're politely herded across the hall into a larger room where rows of folding chairs await. There are programs on the seats, including the agenda and lists of directors and officers. Also included are some meeting rules that seem reasonable enough: no speaking unless recognized by the chairman, three-minute time limits on remarks, no distributing printed materials, and no cameras of any kind. (These guidelines are pretty standard, I'm finding.)

Behind the tables where the presenters are sitting, the curtains over exterior windows are closed. Perhaps that's to minimize distractions—after all, that's *Hawaii* beyond the glass (if only an unspectacular part of downtown Honolulu)—but there's a misty rain falling just now, so maybe not.

Bob Clarke, a tall, young-looking, sixty-year-old wearing a tasteful red Hawaiian shirt, is the corporation's CEO, chairman of the board, and president. He offers an aloha welcome to Hawaiian Electric's 2003 annual meeting and asks how many people traveled from the mainland. I'm one of only 4 of 125 or so shareholders present to raise a hand. As I had learned at Otter Tail's meeting in Fergus Falls, utilities are typically owned by people who live nearby.

Clarke introduces the company's board, then observes that the company's been doing pretty well during a period when most companies haven't been. Of course, the main reason investors bid up Hawaiian Electric's stock price wasn't that it suddenly became a better company. It was that folks who had been badly burned by dot-com flameouts regained their appreciation for stable "old economy" companies with long histories of paying dividends.

Wisely, Clarke does his best to make it clear that the recent price gains were unusual and unlikely to continue. He warns that the company's pension expense liability is increasing faster than the pension fund investments are growing, due to declining interest rates and a struggling stock market. That's bound to cut into next year's profits, he implies; it's a remarkably candid observation of a common problem that most corporations are trying to sweep under the rug. Meanwhile, he notes, an inevitable turnaround in interest rates—currently at all-time lows—will hurt profits at American Savings Bank.

Nobody in the room seems to bat an eyelash. Shareholders in utilities are usually most interested in the dividends—a perennial favorite among retired investors—and that's obviously the case here. Clarke knows it and assures us that the company intends to maintain dividends at the current level for the foreseeable future.

Mike May, the fifty-six-year-old president and CEO of the utility division, takes over. He's wearing a black shirt festooned with golden pineapple images, and somehow it's easy to picture him as a gym teacher.

May says electrical consumption due to tourism is way off because of September 11 and the Iraq War but notes that residential demand is growing. He assures locals that the company routinely holds emergency drills and adds, "Rest assured, service and reliability will never be compromised."

As long as he's on a roll with this reassurance thing, he goes on to proudly point out that Hawaiian Electric ranks in the top 5 percent for "corporate governance," according to the *Wall Street Journal*. That means the company toes the line in a number of ways deemed especially important these days. (For instance, board members must be mostly outsiders—not executives of the company.)

Residents of Hawaii tend to be especially keen on preserving paradise, so May spends some time talking about how the company is testing fuel cells (which draw energy from hydrogen and don't pollute) and how it's building a photovoltaic (solar cell) station in cooperation with the U.S. Navy. He introduces a new "unregulated subsidiary"— smartly named Renewable Hawaii, Inc.—that's been created to seek investors for new environmentally friendly projects. And he says that at Honolulu's Bishop Museum, just down the street, the company is sponsoring a "renewables" exhibit.

That reference to community involvement provides him with an opening to laud the contributions of Hawaiian Electric employees to the Aloha United Way. May served as that organization's chairman in 2002. He makes sure everyone in the room gets the message: This company cares about the community.

Connie Lau, president and CEO of American Savings Bank (ASB), reports on the financial subsidiary's sixth straight year of double-digit income growth. You can tell she's the careful sort by the way she pronounces "Ha-vie-ee" and "Oh-ah-hoo" so distinctly.

Lau, fifty, credits the year's success partly to changes at ASB, which has added investment and insurance services, and partly to great economic conditions for banks. But the low interest rates that encouraged people and businesses to take loans are sure to reverse, she cautions. When they do, some borrowers will pay off their loans early, reducing their interest payments and the bank's potential revenues.

She wraps up with more praise for the Aloha United Way. Then Bob Clarke returns and piles on still more hosannas for the charity. Let no one leave this room without understanding that Hawaiian Electric cares about Hawaii!

It's on that note that Clarke opens the floor to shareholders.

Throughout the meeting, there's been a chubby guy sitting in front of me, rudely rustling papers and muttering. Suddenly he's addressing the executives at the front of the room. From the way he identifies himself, he may or may not be related to one of the country's foremost financial families. He complains, loudly, that Hawaiian Electric's dividend hasn't increased since 1998. Meanwhile, he says, the company has lost millions in ill-fated attempts to do business in China and the Philippines, salaries have gone up, and bonuses have been fat. He grouses that Hawaiian Electric "reminds me a little bit of Enron" and adds, "Somebody should be watching the foxes." Finally he gets to his point. He's willing to be that somebody, to serve as a director "at no charge."

It's bad enough that this guy's in front of me, but suddenly a woman behind me turns into a Greek chorus, repeating his final two words. "No charge," she echoes, flatly.

Clarke reiterates the results investors have enjoyed in recent years, and he points out that pay levels and bonuses are determined solely by outside directors. (If I only had a million bucks for every time I've heard that defense!)

"Outside directors," says the voice behind me.

The questions get easier after that, and sometimes the executives don't even have to open their mouths. When one woman asks if there's any reason other than the dividend that she should buy more Hawaiian Electric stock, another woman chimes in with her belief that the stock price will go higher in time. "You don't lose money in the stock market unless you sell," she says, perhaps forgetting that sometimes people need their money and sometimes companies go bankrupt.

An elderly gentleman says he wonders why the company's chief financial officer had retired last year. Did it have anything to do with him having worked at Arthur Andersen earlier in his career? And, he adds, why were the company's earnings restated?

"Earnings restated," intones the robot behind me.

Clarke looks a bit baffled. He responds that there was nothing unusual after the CFO's departure, and that there had been no restatement of earnings.[1] For good measure, he repeats the company's claim to strong "corporate governance."

"Corporate governance" the voice repeats. I'm beginning to wonder how much damage I could do by jabbing blindly backward with a pen.

---

1. A restatement of earnings is when a company says something like, "Remember when we told you we earned x per share a while back? That was crazy. Turns out those numbers were wrong. We must've been smoking crack or something."

Fortunately, the end is near. A very old Filipino man in the front row rises and begins to walk unsteadily toward the executives. Quickly a Hawaiian Electric employee takes his arm and leads him back to his seat, asking if he'd like to ask a question. Clarke recognizes the man, who beams and asks the audience, "Does everybody have a full stomach? Is everyone happy?" Most people summon up an agreeable grunt in response. The old man goes on to give us a short summary of his life so far, then concludes with an enthusiastic, "The wave of the future is energy, and we have the energy company right here!"

It's hard to imagine a better line to close the meeting. Clarke seizes the moment and calls for adjournment. I sheath my pen and the Greek chorus escapes unharmed to annoy some other people in some other place.

During the elevator ride to the lobby, I hear two shareholders dressed in golf attire talking about another electric company back on the mainland: "Hey, now *there's* a screwed-up utility. Got into cell phones, or something." I'm reminded that many companies go astray by getting into businesses they don't know much about—just as many investors go astray by investing in companies they don't understand.

The next morning, I spend some time talking with Molly Egged, who has been coordinating Hawaiian Electric's shareholder meetings for more than a decade. She's responsible for making sure there are enough chairs and enough coffee and coordinates a group of secretaries who staff the registration area and take care of dimming and raising the lights at appropriate times.

Egged tells me this year's event was pretty typical. The same people tend to ask questions year after year, she says, estimating that three-quarters of the shareholders who show up have been there before. "You wonder if you *don't* see them," she adds.

It's a reminder, of sorts, that we don't all live forever and should try new experiences and enjoy ourselves while we can. At least that's how I choose to interpret it later that day, when I take a free ukulele lesson in a Waikiki shopping mall. Unfortunately, I have no prior musical experience that involves producing a melody, and even the relative simplicity of the four-stringed acoustic uke is lost on me. I quickly realize this is something else that Warren Buffett can do better than I can, so I decline the inevitable offer to purchase one of the instruments.

Just thirty-six hours later, I run into Egged at the shareholder meeting for Alexander & Baldwin, a shipping company that owns a lot of Hawaiian real estate. Still weary from her duties earlier in the week, she sighs and wonders aloud why shareholder meetings are necessary, given that most people don't attend and the votes are usually mere formalities.

She's just letting off a little steam, I think. But at my next stop I meet an investor relations representative who is convinced shareholder meetings should be obsolete.

In a nutshell . . .

HAWAIIAN ELECTRIC

EDUCATIONAL VALUE: **B**
  Admirable candor.
ENTERTAINMENT VALUE: **C**
  A few interesting characters in the crowd.
FREEBIES: **F**
  None.
FOOD & DRINK: **C**
  Breakfast spread included pineapple cake.

INSIGHT: Too many CEOs and company chairmen say everything's coming up roses. Not enough make it a point to tell shareholders, face-to-face, about real issues that could affect future profits. Companies that have been around for a long time often have many retirees drawing pension benefits. If the funds designated to pay those benefits don't grow as fast as the obligations do, the money needs to come from somewhere else—which could mean there will be that much less for the shareholders.

On the Bunny
Side of the Street

PLAYBOY

Disclosure: Perhaps somewhere there really is someone who actually buys Playboy *just for the articles. It's a safer bet that several people have bought shares of the stock just for the pictures; the original certificates included a nude etching of Miss February 1971. Me, I bought the stock because my cousin, who's a pretty sharp investor, suggested that the shareholder meeting might be a hoot. Sadly, I hold my shares in "street name"—mere electronic digits in a brokerage account—so I never see an actual share certificate.*

Where are all the scantily clad Playmates? For that matter, where's the old guy in the bathrobe with the Pepsi in one hand?

You would think Playboy's shareholder meetings might be bacchanalian—all wine, women, and song. But 10:00 on a soggy and cold Chicago morning is too early for wine or song, and there's only one woman starring in this show. Christie Hefner, the founder's fifty-year-old daughter and the company's CEO and chairman of the board since 1988, is very much in charge.

Over the past few years, she's been trying to keep Playboy both relevant and popular. It can't be an easy job, because surely there are those who believe the company's purpose may be to support the founder's rather spectacular lifestyle. Hugh, who still carries the title "Editor in Chief," decamped Chicago for Los Angeles decades ago and has seldom left the opulent Playboy Mansion West since. At any given time, he claims between three to six blonde women in their twenties as his girlfriends and praises Viagra. His exploits are featured on a page or two of "Hef Sightings" each month in the magazine, usually depicting the elderly but well preserved Mr. Playboy cavorting with his current blondes and a bunch of long-ago TV/entertainment/porn stars. It's hard to imagine how this helps efforts to appeal to a younger, hipper audience.

I get a very warm greeting when I check in at Spiaggia, a plush meeting room over a restaurant just a few blocks from Playboy's corporate headquarters. A gorgeous Bunny takes my coat, while a second hands me a martini and a third rubs my shoulders and asks if I had a tough walk over from my hotel. Er . . . okay, I may have imagined everything in that last sentence. In any case, I'm one of just five shareholders present. Everyone else works for the company, in one way or another—and none are centerfold material.

The Playboy folks have no idea why I'm here—probably just another loon thinking he'll cadge an invite to the grotto pool after the meeting, perhaps—but they lead me over to a very elaborate breakfast buffet and introduce me to a few other attendees.

Things are supposed to get under way at 9:30, but that time comes and goes and no one leaves the buffet. I'm reminded of my time in the corporate world, where meetings seldom began until the boss showed up.

At 9:40 Christie Hefner breezes in. You can't miss her: She's wearing a brilliant white suit and has the bearing of someone who knows she must be "on" at all times. She sets up shop behind a lectern as the fifty or so people here quickly take their seats.

Immediately, Hefner announces that she and the directors will stick around for a few minutes after this gathering to answer questions before heading off to a board meeting. It's common enough for a board to meet following a shareholder meeting, but I get the feeling Hefner is telling us that the board meeting is the priority of the day. Also, it seems like she might be establishing an escape route in advance, in case there are any tough questions.

And tough questions are certainly a possibility—or at least they might be if the audience didn't consist almost entirely of Playboy employees who wouldn't dare ask them. Among the items on today's agenda are two company proposals to greatly increase the number of shares used in stock option programs for "key employees" (including the two who serve on the board) as well as "nonexecutive directors" (including the other six directors).

Nobody balks, and nobody asks for a ballot.

That makes life easy for Mike Rimkus, the inspector of elections. Rimkus, who works for a Chicago bank, is responsible for adding up all the votes received beforehand, then reconciling them with any cast at the meeting. He attends about fifteen to twenty shareholder meetings a year. Most of the time there are few votes cast at the meeting itself, so it doesn't take much work to determine the final tallies. Every once in a while the math gets more complicated and he needs to pull a calculator or laptop computer out of his briefcase. "One meeting there were fifteen proposals. A ton of people showed up to vote, and the company wanted the exact totals of votes cast for and against. They had to adjourn for a while to give me time to count the votes," Rimkus explains.

Here at Playboy, Rimkus has a pretty easy job. There's not much doubt about which way the votes will go when the founder still holds nearly 70 percent of the company's stock.

With the voting out of the way, Hefner launches a simple slide presentation reviewing fiscal 2002—a period when the stock price dropped from over thirteen dollars a share to under ten dollars. She seems to be preaching to the choir when she says the stricter financial reporting standards mandated by the recently passed Sarbanes-Oxley Act are especially hard on smaller companies like Playboy. Similarly, everyone here seems to be completely on board with the company's soft-core porn cable projects, including a new twist on reality programming—hypnotizing couples to see what their conflicts and fantasies are, then confronting them with the results. Her claim that the company's rabbit head logo is considered hip by the younger set goes unchallenged. And heads nod as she describes a new clothing store in Tokyo—where dressing room mirrors mimic *Playboy* covers so that when you're trying something on, you can see how you might look *if*.

After a while, Hefner introduces Jim Kaminsky, the new editor of the company's namesake magazine. Kaminsky has just joined *Playboy* from *Maxim*, a U.S. version of British "lad-rags," which tend to feature wiseass photo captions, pictures of hot actresses wearing lingerie, and preposterous tales of male adventures. The genre, which got its start in England, has been a phenomenon, and it's easy to think Playboy hired Kaminsky to keep him from working for the ever-gaining competition.

Not surprisingly, his vision for revitalizing *Playboy* seems to be to make it more like *Maxim*. He wants to focus the monthly Playboy Interview—easily the most respected part of the magazine—on younger subjects, like rap stars. He plans to reduce the use of illustrations because, he says, they don't connect with young readers. And his overall goal is to provide the target audience with "social ammunition"—things to talk about when they're relaxing naked in the hot tub with a martini and at least two members of the opposite sex. I don't hear anything that sounds like it'll set the magazine world on fire, but I may be a lousy judge because I'm too old. Speaking of old, Kaminsky doesn't say a word about "Hef Sightings."

In fact, the patriarch's name is rarely mentioned at all. It seems odd to me at first, but then I realize his absence has a lot to do with why this event is so tame. My theory is that the founder and all of the other shareholders, save for the handful of us in this room, are at this very moment cavorting in the grotto out in Beverly Hills.

After the meeting I spend a few minutes with Martha Lindeman, who handles investor relations. I'm hoping she'll confirm my theory and give me a complimentary grotto pass.

"Where are all the shareholders?" I ask. "Why such a low turnout?"

"The era of annual meetings is over," she declares. "It used to be a wonderful opportunity to get in the horse and buggy and go see what's happening at the company. Of course, a company can use the meeting as a marketing event, but that doesn't make a lot of sense for us."

Over? Horse and buggy? Well, I agree with her about one thing: A shareholder meeting can be useful as a marketing event. In fact, several mutual fund groups that aren't otherwise required to hold shareholder meetings do so anyway for that very reason.

I had been to one such gathering just a week earlier. Southeastern Asset Management—which runs the Long-leaf Partners Funds—attracted more than three hundred investors to the Memphis Botanic Gardens on a night when tornadoes were slicing and dicing the countryside nearby. Attendees were rewarded with a wine-and-cheese reception and genuine gratitude: "We have the best share-holders in the mutual fund business," said Mason Hawkins, Southeastern's tanned and energetic leader.

The food, drink, and compliments were nice, but the main attraction was a Q&A reminiscent of Berkshire's. It even began in pretty much the same way, with the words, "We'll stay as long as you all have questions." It's some-what safer to make that offer at 6:30 p.m. than at 9:00 a.m., of course, but the sentiment went over well nonethe-less. So did the humility of the money managers, who didn't hesitate to admit to mistakes. Hawkins invoked Buffett's name and principles several times—at one point saying, "We don't waste time on stocks where we'll never understand the company's competitive advantage"—so I was surprised when I talked with him after the meeting and learned that he's never been to Omaha in the spring.

Fenimore Asset Management, which runs FAM Funds, holds a similar get-together each October in Cobleskill, New York. It's a beautiful time of year there. The leaves are a riot of autumn colors, and Cooperstown, just down the road, is alive with the buzz of the playoffs and the World Series. When I went to FAM's gathering, the chairman came onstage wearing a safety helmet to under-score what turned out to be the meeting's theme. He defined safety as knowing what you're really invested in—

a good way to put it. Unfortunately, FAM took the safety thing a little too far, scripting the vast majority of the Q&A in advance, with many of the questions being asked by prerecorded voices. The final canned question was one that's on the mind of anyone who plans to be around in the year 2525: "What's your outlook for the next couple of centuries?" The answer, of course, was, "Companies will grow; stocks will go up." On the way out, shareholders received FAM first-aid kits, hammering the theme home one last time.

Of course, several of the obligatory meetings I've attended have been handled with care because the companies see them as investor relations—and even public relations—opportunities. But here at the Playboy gathering, Ms. Lindeman thinks that shareholders can get pretty much all the information they might want or need by accessing conference calls between the company's management and investment analysts. (These calls have been open to individual shareholders since 2000, when the SEC ruled, in "Regulation FD"—for "fair disclosure"—that companies had to make any substantial disclosures of information to all shareholders simultaneously.)

Any individual investor who has ever tried to squeeze a word in on a conference call monopolized by Wall Street analysts could tell her that's hardly the same thing. And when you hang up, nobody hands you a goodie bag filled with a set of coasters, a CD of jazz favorites, and a free copy of the current month's *Playboy*.

After arriving home from Chicago, I sell my Playboy shares at roughly the same price I'd paid for them. It's the first time I've based an investment decision on how I had felt about the shareholder meeting, but I can't shake the idea that Playboy thinks Average Joe and Jane investors aren't much more than a nuisance and that the company exists for the convenience of the few who run it. Shareholders seem to come in second at my next stop, too—but for a very different reason.

In a nutshell . . .

PLAYBOY

EDUCATIONAL VALUE: **C**
   An informative treatment of company's plans.
ENTERTAINMENT VALUE: **F**
   Imagine my disappointment.
FREEBIES: **A**
   Jazz CD, set of coasters, latest issue of *Playboy*.
FOOD & DRINK: **B+**
   Generous breakfast buffet.

INSIGHT: If a company thinks the shareholder meeting has outlived its usefulness, it's easy to turn that view into a self-fulfilling prophecy. Putting on a dull show will discourage return visits—even if the company itself is known for wine, women, and song. When a company is closely held (most shares in the hands of one person or group), management can do whatever it wants. Sometimes going along for the ride can be rewarding; sometimes not. But it's hard to feel like a real partner in the business if the company's representatives point-blank confess that the one day they're supposed to talk with you is a waste of time.

Early Morning Pain

WAL-MART

Disclosure: There's no Wal-Mart especially close to where I live, and I've rarely shopped in a Wal-Mart store, but the world's largest retailer—like an elephant in a room filled with lesser beasts—is impossible to ignore. Its pricing and practices tend to set a standard, and if smaller stores can't compete, well, that's the idea. More than a few small-town Main Street businesses have had to close their doors when Wal-Mart set up shop nearby. Locals often complain but seldom realize the role they play by patronizing the biggest of the big box stores. With mixed feelings, I bought a few Wal-Mart shares in 2002, primarily because I figured the shareholder meeting was a must.

Dawn has barely cracked, here in northwestern Arkansas. Yet at 6:40 a.m. the Bud Walton Arena is roaring with the sound of a live rock group— Guido and the Wal-Mart Band, honest!—doing an oldies set. They're not bad, but my usual response to hearing Grand Funk's "Footstompin' Music" at this insane hour would be to hit the snooze alarm with great satisfaction.

Joe "Guido" Welsh, forty-eight, is the leader of the band, which plays about twenty-five functions each year for the company. He sees himself and his fellow musicians as "cheerleaders with guitars" and merely shrugs at the odd hours: "That's just the gig. It's not rocket surgery." He concedes that singing high notes can be tough first thing in the morning but feels that the most challenging part of his job is probably "writing songs that use words like 'communicate,' 'raising the bar,' and 'teamwork' and making them sound as heartfelt as 'Satisfaction' by the Rolling Stones."

I can't believe I'm here this early. I've come to think of shareholder meetings as mid-morning events and was vaguely prepared for the 8:45 a.m. start shown in the meeting notice. It turns out that was just for the business portion, not for the entire spectacle. Late last night, I spotted the somewhat more aggressive complete schedule in the *Benton County Daily Record*, accompanied by a whopping ninety-six-page full-color supplement all about the Wal-Mart gathering. (It's packed with ads from vendors who either sell to Wal-Mart or would like to, and it dwarfs the paper itself, which typically runs from ten to sixteen pages a day. I've seen several other newspapers devote a page or even an entire section to hyping a local shareholder meeting, but the *Record*'s effort is truly amazing.)

The other fifteen thousand people present here at Wal-Mart's 2003 shareholder meeting are all infuriatingly bright-eyed and relentlessly cheerful. It doesn't take long to figure out why: Nearly all of them seem to be employees of the retail giant. They're wearing color-coded T-shirts identifying the country or division they represent, and sitting in groups waving flags as if they were at the opening ceremonies for the Olympics.

A large, beaming woman wearing a blue "May I Help You?" smock leads me to a seat in a small area set aside for shareholders who aren't employees. I'm just settling in when the band whips into a new tune to get the official festivities under way—the premiere of the official theme song of this meeting, "It's My Wal-Mart."

That phrase is shouted, oh, maybe three or four *hundred* times during the next six hours. Whenever anyone gets onstage (and at one point or another, nearly everyone does), he or she asks, "Whose Wal-Mart is it?" Each and every time, the Wal-Martians respond with proof they've drunk the Kool-Aid.

It's pure sensory overload much too early in the morning, so just before 7:00 a.m. I decide that becoming a coffee drinker for the day might help. There are complimentary doughnuts, muffins, chips, soda, and coffee at the concession stands—and suddenly I understand why the aisles in Wal-Mart stores are so wide.

I fill a plate anyway, just as the lights go down and a terrible bleating begins. Two bagpipers stroll separately through the crowd. When they reach the stage, drums kick in, lights flash, and dry ice fog spews as the duo suddenly starts moonwalking and playing ear-splitting Jimi Hendrix–like riffs. It's so bizarre that it's nearly good.

The crowd loves it and is still roaring its approval as a film begins with an animated comet spreading magic dust around a Wal-Mart store, followed by clips showing the company's operations around the world. Predictably, the associates from each country go wild when their version of Wal-Mart—or its Sam's Club affiliate—is onscreen. The whole place is in a lather when the film ends with a montage of smiling employees.

Just in case anyone has managed to nod off, there's an explosive sound and lights flash as the company's three top executives take the stage. There are no chairs up there, no lecterns—no place to hide. The company has adopted "stand-up" executive meetings (an idea that came from its United Kingdom affiliate, ASDA) as a way of keeping people on their toes, literally, and this is meant to be proof that the idea works.

The three men—CEO and president Lee Scott, executive vice president Tom Coughlin, and chairman Rob Walton, one of legendary founder Sam's sons—stroll around like charismatic TV preachers. Walton is relatively low-key, but the other two seem like they've already had five or six cups of high-test java.

When they speak, it's reminiscent of political representatives who stir up their convention delegates by bellowing, "Mr. Chairman, the Great State of Arkansas, home of that Great American, Sam Walton. . . ." They take turns pandering in twangs that would be right at home on a country music awards show:

"Is there anybody out there from Wal-Mart stores?" (Crowd goes wild.)

"Whose Wal-Mart is it?" (Crowd rips chairs from moorings, sets building afire.)

"Who's Number One?" (Crowd kills and eats visiting writer.)

Sometimes they recycle lines, but the results are always the same. It reminds me of a rock show where the front man keeps shouting, "Wanna hear ya say *yeah!*"

Standing ovations are so common, it's as if there's an endless wave cheer sweeping around the building. Friendly rivalries spring up between crowd contingents as the people in the red T-shirts try to cheer louder than the people in the blue T-shirts, who are trying to cheer louder than the people in the orange T-shirts and so on—like kids at camp.

Scott, who reminds me of a younger Lee Iacocca, fires up the crowd even more—if that's possible—with a real rah-rah about how great a place Wal-Mart is to work and how it's getting better all the time. He introduces a pair of employees from a Wal-Mart store in Mexico, and one of them leads the retailer's official cheer, a spirited recitation of the company's logo. Back in 1992 the hyphen between "Wal" and "Mart" was replaced by a star, but for cheering purposes they still call the non-letter a "squiggly" and wiggle their rear ends when they shout it.

"Gimme a W. . . . Gimme an A. . . . Gimme an L. . . . Gimme a squiggly. . . . Gimme an M. . . . Gimme an A. . . . Gimme an R. . . . Gimme a T. . . . What's that spell? WHAT'S THAT SPELL?" Most of the folks here can probably do the cheer in their sleep (and I pity the bed partners of those who do), but their Mexican colleague leads them through it in Spanish, and some of the audience gets lost. As the Mexicans are leaving the stage, one of the executives jokes, "Yeah, I was right there with you."

Later he says there are eleven hundred Wal-Mart associates here from outside the United States. He adds, "Seventy percent of them don't speak English, so they're listening through headphones to the translators. Let's see if this works. Whose Wal-Mart is it?" He gets a roar in response—much faster than any translator could have reposed the question—and concludes happily, "Guess it works in any language!"

Each time the head of a Wal-Mart division is introduced, a similar trick is employed. "Do we have anyone from *Information Systems* in the house?" shouts one of the executives, prompting a large group way up in the darkened second tier to wave their glowing green necklaces and make a lot of noise.

The gambit falls flat only once. There's almost no response to "Do we have any *cashiers* here?" Perhaps the invitations for hourly wage folks near the bottom of the Wal-Mart totem pole were lost in the mail.

As each division spokesperson bounds onstage, he or she high-fives whoever's already there, then presents the division's "five commitments." There are always five—no more, no less. For the Logistics Division—the group responsible for making sure things get where they're supposed to be, when they're supposed to be there—the five are "service, accuracy, productivity, on-time delivery, and associate development." Even the "People Division," known at most other companies as Human Resources or Personnel, has a list.

I hear so many Top Fives I decide to make one for myself. My Top Five commitments to shareholder meeting research:

1. Pay better attention to start times.
2. Eat a healthy breakfast before leaving the hotel.
3. Bring earplugs in case there are bagpipes.
4. Develop and use self-cheer that includes a "squiggly."
5. Follow Wal-Mart's example and increase my income to the point that it exceeds the GDP of all but a handful of countries.

There are also five overriding commandments for all Wal-Mart employees: "Stock it, price it, show the value, take their money, and teach them." *Take their money?* Well, the Wal-Martians seem to mean it in the nicest of ways.

Listening to the various speakers, I begin to get a feel for the Wal-Mart dialect. It's not just that you have to throw in a Wal-Mart cheer every few minutes and generally adopt a tone that makes it clear whatever you're talking about is the single most interesting topic on the planet. You also need to pepper your sentences with insider references to combinations of letters that are meaningless to outsiders—things like CSMs and VPIs. Most importantly, you need to insert random names at frequent intervals, perhaps on the theory that eventually you'll have acknowledged everyone in your audience. (This is truly weird stuff. It leads to sentences like "The things that we learned, Kevin, are that getting it right, Alice, and doing it fast, Tom, are crucial, Miss Ellen." I'm sure the Kevins and Alices and Toms and Ellens in the crowd are pleased, if a bit mystified. But maybe I'm just miffed because my name never turns up.)

Sprinkled among the divisional reports are winners of Wal-Mart's in-house version of *American Idol.* Drew Mosley, who works in a Sam's Club store in Virginia, wails a gospel tune and gets a standing O. Ezell Clark, an assistant store manager from Fort Worth, gets like recognition for a version of "I'll Always Love You," in which he riffs, winningly, "Wal-Mart, I'll always love you!"

There's professional entertainment, too. Singer Amy Grant (standing O) pops in to play a few songs and announces, "Wal-Mart is a normal part of life for me." While she's the biggest name today, I'm told that country music stars Brooks & Dunn played for the employees earlier in the week. When Grant finishes "Simple Things," a tune that strongly emphasizes those two words by repeating them over and over again, she says, "I drove that title into your forehead with a nail, didn't I? That's what marketing's all about, but I know I'm preaching to the choir." (Another standing O.)

Star sightings aren't rare at Wal-Mart meetings,

although who the stars will be is a secret until showtime. A year earlier, guests had included model Cindy Crawford, actresses Mary-Kate and Ashley Olsen, and football heroes Joe Montana, Johnny Unitas, Dan Marino, and John Elway. Others over the years have included Jessica Simpson, Halle Berry, Bon Jovi, and Garth Brooks. (Wal-Mart is perhaps the only company to encourage shareholders to expect to see celebrities at the annual meeting. At least one company advises its owners to expect just the opposite: The meeting announcement for World Wrestling Entertainment conspicuously states, "Please note that this will be a business meeting only and not an entertainment event. No superstars will be in attendance at the meeting." But it still might be worth going to that one, just in case the directors try to break chairs over each others' heads while the chairman of the board is looking the other way.)

More than two hours after I arrived, I'm still a little lost and beginning to wonder if maybe I've accidentally stumbled into an employee meeting and the shareholder conclave is down the hall. The doubt grows even larger as I watch a flag ceremony take place, with associates from each country in attendance bearing their national flag to the stage. I'm happy to discover that Wal-Mart is content to live with standard geographic conventions, unlike Starbucks.

Lest all the banners confuse anyone, country singer Joe Nichols takes center stage and focuses on the American flag with a heartfelt rendition of the national anthem. It occurs to me that this is probably a transition to the actual business meeting—and so it is, right around 8:45, as promised in the meeting notice. For a fleeting second I wish I had slept in and just turned up now, but then I realize how much I would have missed.

Rob Walton takes over. He seems a little disorganized and more than once says, "Um, let me see here. . . ." I wouldn't be at all surprised if the fumbling is a clever act, though. (For years, I worked with a mutual fund sales executive named Mark Freeman, whose storytelling technique was a wonder to behold. He would typically begin by fooling nervously with his glasses or his notes, then drift into a tale about his brief career as a pitcher in the major leagues. The best of his stories was about a horrible inning one day in 1959 when he and several other hurlers for the Kansas City Athletics managed to give up eleven runs in a single inning—on just one hit by the opposing Chicago White Sox! Somehow, that story always led to a persuasive sales point, although I'm not sure it was ever the same point twice.)

Walton introduces his family—save for his mother, Helen, who hasn't arrived yet—then quickly deflects attention from the fact that he and his relatives own nearly 40 percent of the company's stock (which regularly ranks the family among the ten richest in the world) by asking "Whose Wal-Mart is it?"

"It's *my* Wal-Mart!" the audience responds.

"I can't *hear* you!" he taunts.

"IT'S *MY* WAL-MART!"

He introduces the company's board of directors, which includes John Chambers, CEO and president of Cisco Systems, the Internet router manufacturer that just a few years earlier was the world's largest company but has been badly hurt since by the bust in technology companies. Chambers is leaving the Wal-Mart board after this meeting, citing time constraints.

Wal-Mart's high profile virtually ensures that some people out to change corporate America will decide this is a good place to start. Sure enough, there are seven share-holder proposals on the ballot. Typically, the person chairing the meeting gets the last word before voting begins—one last chance to explain the company's position (and to point out flaws in the opposition's argument or character)—but Walton makes a gracious move, announcing that "in the interest of time, the company will limit its responses to those printed in the proxy statement."

The first three speakers all cite religious affiliations; one, in fact, is a nun. It's not unusual for churches to have strong feelings about the behavior of companies whose stock they hold. A woman representing the Disciples of Christ speaks against genetically modified foods, which, she says, "break the barriers of nature." A minister from a local Unitarian Universalist church, speaking for the Interfaith Center on Corporate Responsibility (which doesn't actually own shares but often presents proposals on behalf of religious institutional investors and "socially responsible" mutual funds), wants the company to favor suppliers with higher labor standards. And Sister Barbara Aires, who is on the Interfaith Center's board, wants Wal-Mart to be more forthcoming about roles for women.

A fourth proposal asks for a more independent board of directors. (Six of the fourteen directors are Walton family members or current or former Wal-Mart executives.)

A fifth urges the board to allow shareholders to vote on the level of interest paid on tax-deferred executive compensation. (This one's confusing enough to make Mom and Pop Shareholders' eyes glaze over, I'm pretty sure. Back in 1993, Congress took away corporate tax deductibility for executive pay over $1 million, unless the excess was based on performance. Many companies, including Wal-Mart, get around that by allowing executives to defer salary over $1 million until they retire. The company pays interest on the deferred amounts, and the interest rate has been, some say, generous.)

A sixth proposal also deals with executive pay, seeking to index stock option grants to corporate profits—in other words, to reward people for a job well done, rather than just for showing up.

A seventh proposal requests that the company use a different company to audit the financial reports than it uses for other accounting work.

Rob Walton interrupts only twice—once to explain that the board is already planning to move to having two-thirds of the directors be outsiders, and the other time to introduce his mother, who's just arrived. Helen Walton, the founder's widow, has people on each side holding her up. There's a smile glued to her face as if it's the only expression she's able to manage. It's perfect for the moment: she gets the loudest cheers of the day, and with this crowd that's really saying something.

After the proposals there's another parade of executives playing show-and-tell and filling up the time needed to collect and tally ballots from the handful of shareholders who've chosen to vote in person.

John Menzer, who heads Wal-Mart International, talks up George clothing, a private-label brand from the United Kingdom—and demonstrates how hip it is by having four models strut around the stage.

David Glass, who is Scott's predecessor as CEO and president, wanders into the wayback machine and offers, "I think that this meeting is unique. All of us in the company welcome the shareholders of the company and we work for them. When I went to business school, we were taught that shareholder meetings were held in out-of-the-way places, where not many people could come. From the beginning, we swam upstream."

Hmmm. I suppose it's remotely possible that Fayetteville is less out-of-the-way than nearby Bentonville, where the company's headquarters are located. But you'd have a hard time proving it's easy to get here from the outside world.

A group of executives gathered onstage tries Red Bull, a caffeinated energy drink they're pushing at Sam's Club. Either they're sipping live scorpions, or else they're hamming up their reactions just a bit.

Guido and the Wal-Mart Band do a bit of "Takin' Care of Business" before chief financial officer Tom Schoewe brings the crowd up to date on allegedly exciting accounting developments.

Lee Scott introduces actress Karen Duffy (whose movie credits include *Reality Bites* and *Dumb & Dumber*) plus football star Jay Novacek, and finally, his own wife. All of which leads to several more standing Os. Things go on long enough that a "retrospective" look at the company actually includes a slide of Scott's presentation just a few hours before! Finally, Walton reports that all of the shareholder proposals have failed, but he concedes that several got more than 20 percent favorable votes.

Then he adjourns the official meeting and turns the audience over to a young blonde named Diana DeGarmo, Miss Teen Georgia for 2002. She belts out a version of "Crazy," holding some notes long enough to make Celine Dion sound like a slacker, then does a credible "Over the Rainbow." After the musical visit to Oz, the band picks up the tempo as DeGarmo enlists Coughlin, Scott, and another executive to be her dancers while she wails "Chain of Fools." Everyone in the crowd is up and clapping along—and laughing at how little rhythm the big bosses have.

Finally, after noon, the troops are dismissed and the nonemployees are invited down to the stage to mingle with the executive team and ask questions. A few hundred take advantage of the offer. I'm impressed at how thoughtfully the Wal-Mart bigwigs deal with problems large and small. When a farmer from Texas comments about loose shopping carts at a Wal-Mart near him, it gets every bit as much attention as complaints that Americans are losing jobs because so many products Wal-Mart sells are made in China.

I spend a few minutes chatting with Gene Devaux, a retiree from Missouri, who tells me that his son-in-law once worked for Wal-Mart but discovered it paid better to do the same job as an outside consultant. Devaux says he asks a question or two every year and thinks the shareholder meeting provides an ideal forum: "You can call 'em, but you'll get more action here." It's the sort of thing I had hoped to hear a shareholder say somewhere along the line. I tell him I'm writing a book about shareholder meetings.

When he hears that, he insists I should meet Rob Walton, and next thing I know he's introducing me to the billionaire chairman. Walton tells me how the company's shareholder meetings have evolved and concedes that the event I've just seen was really aimed at employees: "We had the first year's meeting [after the company went public in 1970] at a little hotel in Little Rock. There wasn't a soul there. We needed the investment bankers and analysts [Wall Street types], so we started to treat them to a nice weekend—golf outings, tennis tournaments, and a float trip we still have. That was the focus. Over the years, it's shifted to associates. We take care of the business we should, but it's an opportunity to bring them in and have a bit of fun."

It's early afternoon when I leave the arena. I'm not sure what to do with the rest of the day, but it occurs to me that it might be interesting to check out the local Wal-Mart. When I get there, I'm barely able to find a parking space, because the lot's filled with every inflatable product mascot imaginable. It looks like the staging era for a Macy's Thanksgiving parade. There's a Keebler Elf who must be twenty feet tall. There's a monstrous pink Energizer Bunny, tethered to the ground. There's a huge replica of a dairy cow appendage hovering overhead on behalf of a lotion called Udderly Smooth Udder Cream.

Beneath the balloons are stands offering free food—onion rings, fries, catfish, and sodas, so there's no danger anyone will overdose on nutrients. Parked smack in the middle of things is a racecar with a very loud engine that someone keeps revving, luring people to the already-long lines for several NASCAR track simulators. Scattered around the lot are product representatives handing out free samples, including an engine treatment in the sort of packet that fast-food restaurants use for ketchup and mustard.

It's been a long day and I'm Wal-Marted out. As I leave, I grab a soda and a few sample cans of cat food for my furry friends back home. My suitcase is already crammed tight and these won't help a bit, but I can't resist. After all, freebies are few and far between these days—as I'll soon

be reminded at the shareholder meeting of one of the
world's richest companies.

In a nutshell . . .

WAL-MART

EDUCATIONAL VALUE: **B**
　Solid explanations of the world's largest retailer.
ENTERTAINMENT VALUE: **A**
　Rock 'n' roll, celebrities, films, inflatable mascots.
FREEBIES: **D**
　Soda and pet food samples at local Wal-Mart store.
FOOD & DRINK: **C**
　Free coffee and doughnuts.

INSIGHT: A half-time rally? A political convention? A rock
concert? A religious revival? Yes, on all counts!

10

Butterflies Aren't Free

MICROSOFT

Disclosure: My first personal computer was a Mac, and I was an Apple loyalist until 1997, when I waved the white flag, bought a PC, and eventually picked up some Microsoft shares. In 2004, fatigued by fighting spam and computer viruses, I went back to a Mac. But I kept my Microsoft shares, knowing my defection wouldn't make a dent in the company's market dominance. If only I'd known that the iPod was coming along. . . .

"There will be vats in the lobby filled with complimentary computers, stock options, and antitrust lawsuit settlements," I assure my pal who's taken the day off from his job in nearby Seattle to join me at Microsoft's 2003 shareholders meeting.

I'm lying. Oh, there are giveaways, but they're hardly worth taking away. One is a big red, white, and blue button that says, "Support the right to innovate." It touts a "grassroots" lobbying organization whose Web address just happens to be the same as Microsoft's. The other freebies are a sign-up disk for MSN Internet service and a demo disk of "Amazing Things" you can do with Windows XP (unless your PC, like mine, is too old to play the disk).

As it turns out, Bill Gates may be the world's richest man, but he's a little tight when it comes to welcoming Microsoft's shareholders. The venue is dreary, the stage is nearly bare, and the coffee-and-Danish buffet is meager.

Most unnerving, though, is the "company store," flogging stuff emblazoned with the MSN butterfly and other Microsoft logos. It's doing a brisk business with shareholders who have tech nerds on their holiday gift lists. Butterfly Beanie Babies are hot sellers. Unattractive button-down shirts featuring the Microsoft Office logo seem somewhat less popular. Among the more unusual logo items offered are lunchboxes, golf tees, and even cell phone battery chargers.

This sort of stuff doesn't bother me at Berkshire Hathaway's meeting, because it doesn't seem so shameless there. Warren Buffett lives in the same relatively ordinary house he bought in Omaha for $31,000 in 1958; these days it's assessed at about $700,000. Bill Gates's house, in nearby Medina, Washington, is anything but ordinary (it's fifty thousand square feet plus garages and outbuildings), and the property taxes alone run a million bucks a year. On the other hand, Gates does have more money than Buffett, and he's given away billions, through his foundation, to educational and global health-related causes (especially the eradication of malaria).[1]

The oddest item here among all the crassness is an "answer ball," based on the Magic 8-Ball toy that superstitious kids have enjoyed for generations. Microsoft's version is perhaps appropriately flawed: The screen often goes blank, and messages that do appear (such as "Indications say yes,"

---

1. Buffett began divesting his fortune in 2006 by making annual gifts to Gates's foundation.

"Unlikely," and "Absolutely") are difficult to read. But there must be *something* paranormal in the air, because another shareholder reads my mind when he picks up one of the answer balls, examines it briefly, and muses aloud, "This must be what they use to make the big decisions at Microsoft."

It's an observation that may well have been noted with distaste at very high levels, because just then the Gershwinesque music that had been playing through the PA system stops suddenly and a slightly ominous voice thunders: "Ladies and gentlemen, please take your seats. We are ready to begin."

Four of the people who make the calls at Microsoft are seated behind a plain table at the front of the room: John Connors (chief financial officer), Brad Smith (the company's top lawyer), Steve Ballmer (CEO), and Bill Gates (chairman and "chief software architect"). All are middle-aged white guys wearing dull suits—a description that also covers most of the fifteen hundred or so shareholders present.

Usually the chairman or CEO—often the same person—runs the show at a shareholder meeting. Here it's Connors who guides the proceedings. He talks about how the economy's been stinko but Microsoft has done okay anyway, recording double-digit revenues. What's more, he says, there's been "good progress resolving litigation against the company." That, of course, is a reference to the various antitrust cases against Microsoft, including one in Europe so hot that Brad Smith will be leaving for Brussels right after this meeting.

Gates—a surprisingly small man, who's rocking back and forth nervously, as if he would rather be anywhere else—is ostensibly here just to deliver a technology update. Yet he's the person all the shareholders are watching. It's easy to forgive Scott Weinberg of the Population Research

Institute, who ignores everyone else in the room when he begins presenting a shareholder proposal by saying, "Mr. Gates, it's an honor to be here." (The proposal is to stop Microsoft from making charitable donations, because some of the money might end up in the hands of people who feel differently than Weinberg does about abortion, cloning, and the use of embryos in research. Fewer than 2 percent of votes cast favor the proposal.)

Gates, delivering his report on how he thinks Microsoft will change the world in the next twelve months, is full of geek hyperbole. He observes that the company spent a whopping $6.8 billion on research and development during the past year. What's all that cash bought?

Well, there's Dot Net, which Gates had defined in 2002 as "software to connect information, people, systems, and services," all under a Microsoft umbrella. "We believed our standards would prevail and our level of interoperability would help the industry solve problems," Gates says. But it turned out that people didn't trust Microsoft to, among other things, serve as a repository of credit card information.

Mostly, though, there's continuing work on the long-awaited "Longhorn," an all-new operating system that's supposed to be a big improvement over Windows. Gates can barely contain himself as he describes "the most empowering tool that's ever been created." It makes me wish I had been around to see the inventors of the wheel, the lever, and fire tout their creations to the unsuspecting masses.

I notice that the friend I dragged along has fallen asleep—perhaps an understandable response to big promises from a company with a long record of selling products that sometimes seem to hamper productivity at least as much as they increase it. But Gates's pitch apparently left one attendee breathless, because when Connors returns he announces that medical help has been summoned and the unfortunate man "is conscious and breathing." (Although the average age of shareholders attending annual meetings is at least sixty-five, this was the only medical emergency I saw throughout my odyssey.)

Ballmer, up next, is a stout, balding drill sergeant–type, who gives the impression that anyone who dares question Microsoft is in some way unpatriotic. "We have to make people understand the incredible value that comes on one tiny CD!" he shouts. Yes, shareholders will certainly benefit if Microsoft does well, but Ballmer's talking to us like we're employees rather than co-owners.

Ballmer, who was Gates's dorm mate at Harvard, became Microsoft's CEO in 2000 when Gates decided to step aside and focus on developing technology rather than running the business. (Ballmer is the first person ever to become a billionaire based on stock options received as an employee rather than a founder or a founder's relative, but he and Gates stopped accepting options years before Microsoft abolished its program in 2003. Neither needed the money, of course: Ballmer's only twenty-three places behind Gates among the world's richest men, according to *Fortune* magazine's 2006 tally.)

During the Q&A, a representative of a pension fund that owns shares in Microsoft has a few questions about the company's stock options program, approved by shareholders earlier in the meeting. He wants to know how and why Microsoft would award up to fifty million options and what could possibly justify giving up to twenty million of them to any one person. Ballmer responds, "We don't expect to grant all fifty million but wanted flexibility. Twenty million to anyone would be a lot with the stock at twenty-six dollars a share"—he knocks on wood—"but the stock could vary up and down, and the price will probably be considered when grants are made."

A former Microsoft employee who claims to have suffered a repetitive stress injury from excessive mouse manipulation wonders how common his situation is. Brad Smith quickly offers the corporate lawyer's take: He's "not aware that it's widespread," and "Microsoft's [safety] policies exceed those of Washington state." Gates adds, "As speech recognition gets better and better, the opportunities to minimize mouse use will increase." (Speech recognition programs still make me nervous. Maybe that's because I recently spent too long trying to convince an airline's voice-prompted reservations system that I wanted to go to Austin, not Boston.)

The big question of the day, though, is whether Microsoft will get serious about returning some of its $50 billion+ cash hoard to shareholders. The company began paying a small dividend in 2003, but that hasn't been enough to satisfy investors. After all, this is a company that made a lot of people rich in the 1980s and the 1990s, yet the stock price has been relatively flat since 2001. Connors hides behind the ongoing antitrust cases and says, "We have significant legal issues that should be resolved before making significant changes to dividend policy." It's a pat answer. Few believe that the company would be hurting for cash even if it had to pay several large settlements.

The complaint that shareholders aren't getting much back from the company can't be ignored, and Ballmer knows it. Wrapping up, he points out that parking is free for shareholders attending the meeting—if, that is, they parked directly under the building (which we didn't). I'm struck by the irony of a company fighting charges that it's a *monopoly* associating itself with *free parking*.

Few attendees on their way out bother to check out the product-demo kiosks in the back of the room, hosted by bright young people tossing around tech terms I'll never understand—and passing along questionable information. At the Spam Elimination booth, for instance, we're told that spam from overseas can be controlled effectively by relying on local laws.

The Xbox booth, pushing Microsoft's electronic game system, attracts only a few wandering ten-year-olds bent on "driving" a Porsche at high speed through the streets of Barcelona. After they've quickly mastered the weird Xbox joystick, which features no fewer than eleven different buttons, the kids look bored.

At the investor relations booth, I ask whether this morning's meeting was broadcast on the Internet and learn that the audio was live but the video was on a one-hour delay for (you guessed it) cost reasons. I have to give Microsoft credit for trying. When I first considered coming to this meeting, I was stunned to discover that the company's Web site included a complete transcript of the previous year's meeting. But that was just words onscreen, and an audio feed of the meeting is just a soundtrack. Nothing short of a live video feed can help investors see if the rascals running their companies flinch at tough questions (and even then the cameras would need to be in the right places at the right times).

The cost of such technical features is coming down all the time. Cisco Systems offered live audio and video of its 2005 meeting.

There are, of course, any number of companies that would love to go one step further and hold the meeting only in cyberspace. It's an idea that's legal for companies chartered in Delaware—but perhaps not an idea whose time has come. In 2003 software maker Siebel Systems proposed a Web-only meeting, but angry shareholders insisted on getting together the old-fashioned way.

If a huge, widely traded technology leader like Microsoft can't make the most of the Internet at shareholder meeting time, what chance does a tiny, thinly traded company in a decidedly low-tech industry have? To find out, I need to spend some time with people who hang out in alleys.

In a nutshell . . .

MICROSOFT

EDUCATIONAL VALUE: **C**
    Tech talk, no translation headphones provided.

ENTERTAINMENT VALUE: **D**
    Boring. The friend I brought along napped.

FREEBIES: **F**
    MSN sign-up disks, parking—if you knew where.

FOOD & DRINK: **D**
    Very meager breakfast buffet.

INSIGHT: Just because a company has a lot of money doesn't mean it'll bring out the fine china when the shareholders come to town. My wife thinks it's crazy that people will pay for logo T-shirts, which turn the whole notion of paid advertising upside-down. I'm not quite as averse to the concept and have purchased more than a few billboard T-shirts or similar goods that somehow rubbed me the right way. I just don't see how anyone can feel warm and fuzzy enough about a humorless monolith to keep its gift-shop cash registers ringing.

11

(I'm In With)
The Pin Crowd

BOWL AMERICA

Disclosure: Years ago, I was a reasonably good bowler. It's not the sort of accomplishment that will further a nonbowling career, but there's a certain satisfaction in knowing you can hold your own in an alley (especially if you're hopeless at every other sport). Once, I even pulled off bowling's most difficult shot. With my first ball, I had left just the two outside pins in the back row standing—a dreaded outcome known as a seven-ten split.[1] I aimed my second ball to take out just one of the two loafers and turned around after launching it, confident I would end up with a score of nine for the frame. So I never saw the ten-pin dive across the lane and kick the seven just hard enough to knock it down, too. These days, I never turn around until the pins are done falling. Although the popularity of bowling waxes and wanes, I don't feel the need to pay such close attention to my stock in Bowl America—a tiny company that operates eighteen bowling centers in the Washington, D.C., metropolitan area and in Florida, and has increased its quarterly dividends for more than three decades.

---

1. This would also be a bad thing for a stock! A seven-ten split in stock terms would mean that the company took your ten shares and gave you seven back. It would be a "reverse split," which is what desperate companies sometimes do when they want to increase their share price quickly. In most situations, the numbers are more like one-ten—so you'd get one share for every ten you had, and that one would be worth ten times as much. As Rocky the Flying Squirrel often said, "Hey, Bullwinkle, that trick NEVER works." Companies that do reverse splits almost invariably seem to go bankrupt anyway.

W hile the dozen or so investors attending Bowl America's 2003 shareholder meeting are dapper for the occasion, they would be every bit as comfortable wearing shirts with their names stitched over the pockets and two-toned shoes that slide just so. Me, too. It's only 10:00 a.m., but on the lanes right next door to the company's Alexandria, Virginia, headquarters, bowlers are already knocking down pins (seldom as many as they'd like). For us, such pleasures will have to wait.

My suspicion that the annual get-together for this small chain of bowling centers in Virginia, Maryland, and Florida might be a bit unusual proves to be well founded. The call to order comes from a blast on a whistle blown by Leslie Goldberg, the company's chairman. Other shareholders and directors wind up conversations about life in Palm Beach or thereabouts. I finish filling out a door prize entry slip, grab a powdery doughnut from a giant platter of bowler chow, and take a seat in one of the twenty or so folding chairs set up in the foyer.

Goldberg—a tall, thin man in his midseventies—is clearly a playful sort. He compliments one of the female board members on her scarf, which features bowling pins. Then he works the legally required stuff in between amusing tales from Bowl America's early days.

His parents, Eddie and Ida, enjoyed bowling during the Depression and founded the company with a group of friends in 1958. One of their first employees was a cost-conscious administrator known as Mrs. Darby, whose frugality established a standard the company still holds dear.

"Once, a vendor asked Mrs. Darby why she was rolling up a used adding machine tape rather than throwing it away," Goldberg says. "She looked at him like he was crazy and explained, 'We need to use the other side!'" The story is met with appreciative laughter, and I realize that everyone in the room is old enough to have spent years working with adding machines before calculators became commonplace.

For that matter, everyone here would probably be quite capable of scoring pin-falls manually, without the help of a computer—and they might even prefer to go that route. The old-style score sheets, Goldberg points out, were numbered and served as receipts back when the accounting system depended on pieces of paper in a cigar box.

"And that worked very well," he adds, "except for one time when at the end of a reporting period the books were off by a dime. The accountants went through everything over and over again and kept coming up ten cents short. I offered to put in the dime myself to make the books balance, but everyone objected. They kept looking, and four hours later they found the dime!" Okay, maybe it wasn't the most efficient way of handling the situation, but it speaks volumes about integrity.

Just in front of me, two young men in suits laugh. They're from accounting giant Deloitte & Touche, which serves as Bowl America's independent auditor—in charge of examining and verifying the company's financial records—and they're here to answer questions, if any. Goldberg's stories make it clear that Bowl America worries about the pennies (or at least the dimes), making an auditor's job during the rest of the year relatively simple.

Goldberg's not the only one with interesting tales from the past. A shareholder gets into the spirit of things and recalls that when he was a pin boy in Chicago in the early 1940s, bowlers who had rolled a good game would toss a quarter down the alley, as a tip.

When the reminiscing is finished, Goldberg fires up a

laptop and shows us how Bowl America is making use of the Internet. One of the company's two Web sites keeps league members in touch with one another. The other site is an interactive bowling party planner that has brought in so much business in just a few weeks that one alley manager has asked if they might give it a rest, Goldberg explains with a grin.

Goldberg goes on to talk up the company's two "Rolling Bowling" trucks (semis with real lanes and automatic pin-setters in the trailers) that visit area schools to promote the game, and a promotion that entitles students to a free game for every A on their report cards. He also introduces new cash-balance gift cards, then announces that one of us will be going home with a twenty-five-dollar card, today's door prize. When it turns out to be me, I realize I now have a new standard for "favorite souvenir from a shareholder meeting."

Typically the directors of a company sit out in the audience at shareholder meetings—often toward the front, so they can be seen when the chairman asks them to stand and take a bow. At Bowl America, the directors—a decidedly gray but lively bunch that includes Goldberg's sister—are all at the table up front facing the rest of us. It's a very nice touch and makes me feel they understand the concept of accountability.

Mostly, though, they're accountable to themselves, because the members of the board own nearly 70 percent of the outstanding shares. (If you've ever wanted to sit on a corporate board, one of the best ways to get there is to buy a big, big chunk of the company's stock.)

It's relatively unusual for a small company primarily owned by a handful of investors to have publicly traded shares. It's probably even more unusual for such a company to not do a lot of grousing about the costs of complying with the Sarbanes-Oxley rules requiring more detail in financial reports, but there's no whining here.

At the end of the meeting, one of the directors announces that it's Goldberg's seventy-fourth birthday and leads us all through a verse of the song commonly sung on such occasions (no, not "Proud Mary Keep on Bowlin'"). That's followed by a friendly invitation to dig into a cake waiting nearby, and to have more than one slice.

I spend a few minutes talking with Goldberg between forkfuls and tell him that I was impressed with today's meeting. I'm even more impressed by his aw-shucks response: "Well, you have to remember that as of yesterday the stock was at an all-time high. Nobody's mad about anything."

He worries aloud that the stock may seem more attractive than it should, since the P/E ratio (the stock's price divided by the company's earnings) is artificially low. That's because the company sold a property, and accounting rules require that the proceeds be considered earnings. "I've seen a lot of people buying a hundred shares at a crack, and I hope they're not getting in at the wrong time," Goldberg says with disarming honesty. Because Bowl America is so thinly traded—only a few hundred shares are bought and sold each day, on average—even a single transaction can have a significant affect on the share price.

As I put my coat on, I hear a woman telling Goldberg that a friend's daughter recently held a wedding rehearsal dinner at a Bowl America outlet and "it was a fabulous night." Without missing a beat, Goldberg responds, "Next year, a wedding!"

I leave thinking this might be the most educational

and enjoyable shareholder soirée east of Omaha. I'm reinvigorated and can hardly wait to see what's waiting at the next stop on the annual meeting trail. It turns out to be a lynch mob.

In a nutshell . . .

BOWL AMERICA

EDUCATIONAL VALUE: **A**
   Strong overview of company operations.
ENTERTAINMENT VALUE: **B**
   Amusing historical stories kept things rolling.
FREEBIES: **A**
   $25 gift card (if you won the door prize, like I did).
FOOD & DRINK: **C**
   Coffee, doughnuts, birthday cake. (What? No beer?)

INSIGHT: Tiny gems are more difficult to find than big ones, but they're out there. It's possible for a thinly traded and closely held company to treat individual investors as welcome partners. Especially when the number of shareholders is relatively small, the annual meeting can provide outstanding access to the company's executives, and Q&A sessions can be genuine conversations.

Hey Mickey, Not So Fine

DISNEY

Disclosure: When I was a kid, a trip to Walt Disney World, in Orlando, was a near-annual treat. As an adult living in Los Angeles, I got to the Magic Kingdom even more frequently. I've always been impressed by the high standards at the theme parks—and at the amounts of money people spend when they visit. But I never felt any urge to buy Disney stock until late 2003, when it became clear that the 2004 shareholder meeting would feature a remarkable showdown.

What is it about Pennsylvania and big rats? The most lingering image I have from Hershey's shareholder meeting is the inflatable rodent an angry union used to send a message.

Here in Philadelphia for the 2004 Disney shareholder meeting, I'm seeing big rats all over the place. Last night, just before I turned out the lights in my embarrassingly seedy hotel room around the corner from the convention center, I looked into the alley three stories down and saw several members of Mickey and Minnie's exceedingly well-fed advance team scooting around the very building I was about to sleep in.

This morning, strolling through the lobby of the convention center, I pass through another infested area. In this instance, though, the critters are huge statues of Mickey—seventy-five of them—decorated by celebrities.

Those aren't the only Disney characters to be seen. There are several folks in costumes wandering around outside, including a Cinderella who is strolling among cars stopped in morning rush-hour traffic. Whether these folks are actually on Disney's payroll is anybody's guess.

If they're merely exhibitionists, they couldn't have chosen a better venue. For months, two former members of Disney's board—Roy Disney (Walt's nephew) and Stanley Gold (who is president and CEO of Shamrock Capital Advisors, Roy's investment firm)—have been leading a very visible campaign to dethrone longtime CEO and chairman of the board Michael Eisner. The media is eating it up. This morning I turned on the TV as soon as I woke and discovered that CNBC had moved to Philly for the day to cover the meeting.

Anticipating quite a crowd, Disney had specified in the meeting notice that shareholders could bring only one guest, that admission would be first-come, first-served, and that registration would begin at 8:00 a.m.—two hours before the meeting itself! I want to be sure of a seat, so I skip breakfast to stand in line. Actually, I figure that Disney will provide some sort of food, like most companies do. I'm wrong. There's coffee and orange juice, but no breakfast. So far my experience with shareholder meetings has been that they seldom last more than an hour or two—Berkshire Hathaway's excepted—so I figure I'll be able to hold out until lunchtime.

Given Disney's much-vaunted crowd-control capabilities (you can't help but be impressed by the way the theme parks make long waits tolerable), it's shocking how chaotic the lines are here. Could it be that they wouldn't mind if shareholders got discouraged, gave up, and went home?

Nobody's going to. Every one of the three thousand or more shareholders present wants to see how Michael Eisner handles himself in what will surely be, for him, The Unhappiest Place on Earth. There's every reason to believe, based on early reports about votes already received, that at least a third of shareholders won't cast their ballots in favor of reelecting Eisner to the board. It's unusual for directors to receive anything less than an overwhelming mandate, so the opposition to Eisner is expected to send a strong message.

Ironically, when I finally get inside the meeting room, the PA system is playing the happy-go-lucky "Just a Spoonful of Sugar (Helps the Medicine Go Down)."

The auditorium is huge and it's lit up like a crime scene, thanks, in part, to all the TV crews. I work my way around a few more of those giant decorated rodents and find a seat next to an analyst for a fund that tries to profit from mergers; he's here because cable giant Comcast has announced it might try to acquire Disney (as if Eisner doesn't have enough headaches just now).

The crowd is younger than I'm used to seeing; the average age might be forty. Most eyes are on the three screens at the front, where an old cartoon is showing Mickey Mouse conducting an orchestra through a storm as the musicians tumble about. I can't help but wonder if it's supposed to be sending some sort of message about how Eisner continues to lead despite the current uproar. When the cartoon is over, everyone expects Eisner to appear. Instead, another perverse—maybe even cocky—tune comes from the PA system: "Who's Afraid of the Big Bad Wolf?"

When the beleaguered executive does take the stage, it's easy to tell where his friends and relatives are seated. The only applause seems to come from the left side of the room.

Eisner, who is hoarse, starts things off by pointing out that Disney's stock is up 60 percent in the most recent year. He doesn't mention that the gain only brings the price back to where it was two years earlier—and anyone who had invested three years ago is still down 50 percent.

He admits that results from two major subsidiaries, ABC and Disney Stores, have been disappointing. And he explains that the reason Disney hasn't renewed its agreement with Pixar—the animation company responsible for *Finding Nemo*, among other titles—is that "the economics of the ongoing relationship were not in the best interests of our shareholders."

Eisner tries to build the groundwork to defend himself. He says that Disney's board "has taken a leadership role in contemporary corporate governance" and introduces former senator George Mitchell, who is the lead director.

Mitchell does a long golly-gee-we're-honest-and-omniscient pitch before giving Roy Disney and Stanley Gold fifteen minutes to speak their minds. The lights pan to the right, several hundred feet from—and several feet below—the main stage. There, at a lectern on the floor, are the renegades. The crowd whoops and many rise to their feet. Applause eats up at least one of the allotted minutes.

Gold, a long-faced man in his early sixties, complains that the board hasn't penalized Eisner for any number of expensive mistakes. "While shareholders have watched earnings decline, Michael Eisner has *never* had a bad year!" he observes. He says the vote against reelecting

Eisner to the board will be "an unprecedented vote of no confidence in the annals of American business." He insists, "Michael Eisner must leave *now*," and vows, "If this board fails to act, we will be back."

Roy Disney looks a lot like his famous uncle. While Gold is all business, Disney, in his midseventies, is all sly, small-town charm—exactly what you would expect from someone with his last name. He shows his smarts right away, pre-empting any effort to limit his remarks by saying, "I hope if we run a little long, they won't shut off the microphone."

Then Disney shows his passion for the company. It "is more than just a business," he says. "It's an authentic American icon. It's real, meaningful, and worthwhile to millions all over the world." He's disappointed by the level of quality and creativity shown in recent projects, and he blames Eisner. "I don't believe that art and artists are commodities," he says, adding that he prefers the Disney *name* to the Disney *brand*. "Brands are something you do to cows. They're useful to ranchers. Branding is what you do when there's nothing original about your products."

Eisner returns to a smattering of applause from his supporters and counters, "You have just heard rhetoric from our critics—a disservice to our cast members [Disney employees] and our shareholders." It's a perfect example of how Eisner's approach has angered a lot of people.

When Eisner asks if there are any questions or comments from shareholders regarding nominations for the company's board—including the seat he holds—a familiar voice responds. "If I am the queen, you are the king!" Evelyn Davis teases. She rambles on in her inimitable way for a few minutes, somewhere along the line saying she's an Eisner supporter. That may buy her another thirty seconds or so, but eventually even Eisner tires of the performance and says, "I don't want to cut you off, because you voted for me, but wrap it up."

Davis shouts, "I have one more question!" The crowd, almost as one, shouts, "No!" Davis keeps yelling. Eisner says, "I thought Stanley was difficult." For a minute, I almost feel sorry for him. Then I realize he's probably pleased with Davis's antics, because they provide some comic relief from the main event.

A Disney "cast member" who might be angling for a raise says she's a "lowly producer" at ABC but has always been able to e-mail Eisner with her creative ideas and receive a personal response. Eisner responds: "It's a tough world and you need a tough CEO." The exchange smells like a setup.

It's hard to believe he's still campaigning, because it's unimaginable that anyone is still undecided about voting for or against him. Actually, it's impossible to vote "against" Eisner or any board nominee. Choices are limited to "for" or "withheld," and whoever gets the most "for" votes wins. Of course, there's almost always exactly the same number of candidates—people who tend to either own a big chunk of the company or play golf with someone who does—as seats, so a single "for" vote can suffice (although some companies do require a majority of the votes that are cast).[1] It's reminiscent of the way the Kremlin used to do things.

---

1. If buying a lot of shares doesn't elicit an invitation to join the board, there are ways to force the issue. In 2002 a fund manager bought nearly a third of Pizza Inn's shares, then refused to attend the shareholder meeting or to vote his shares. Without his participation there was no quorum, so the board had little choice but to ask him to become a director. But "proxy fights"—where individuals try to nominate themselves—can be prohibitively expensive to mount. After all, the board can spend company money to fight such challenges, while individual shareholders must dig into their own pockets.

The always-exciting issue of whether to approve the outside auditor suggested by the board is seldom in doubt for pretty much the same reason: no competition. That doesn't stop Davis from asking a few questions. "Which parts of the company are making money?" she asks, only she uses maybe a hundred times as many words to get to the same place. The question itself is certainly fair, but one that's sure to be covered in detail later on. Eisner assures her, "We'll get to that." Not good enough for Davis, who bristles, "Don't tell the accountants not to answer me!" Eisner relents, turns to the auditor's representative, and says, "If you can understand the question, you answer it."

Gamely, the accountant gives it a try. Amazingly, the answer seems to satisfy Davis, for the moment. Eisner tells us that shareholders who haven't already mailed in their ballots have one last opportunity to cast their votes—and that the results will be announced at the end of today's meeting.

That's if it ever *does* end. There are plenty of folks in the audience who have something to say. Davis has a few more questions and, of course, wants to plug her own appearance later that day on CNBC. A woman who collects Disney merchandise offers starry-eyed praise for how it's given her life meaning. When another woman objects to that same merchandise being made in China, Eisner makes the mistake of temporarily turning around, and she roars, "I'm talking to you—not the back of your head!"

Then for the next four hours or so, there's a parade of midlevel executives who file reports from increasingly obscure parts of the Disney universe.

Around lunchtime, my stomach begins to demand

attention. By 1:30 it's complaining loudly. Although everyone onstage disappears at one point or another long enough to grab a bite, there's evidently no plan to feed the shareholders. Or rather there is a plan—*not* to feed the shareholders, in hopes that we'll go away before the vote is announced.

By 2:00 half of the crowd has given in to hunger pangs (and/or sheer exhaustion) and deserted the meeting. By 3:00 the place looks like Dodger Stadium after the seventh inning, when most Angelenos bolt in an effort to beat the traffic. I'm starving, but I don't want to miss what promises to be the climactic moment of the day.

At 3:20 Eisner finally attempts to wrap things up— without taking care of one crucial bit of business. A shareholder shouts a demand to hear the results of the vote. Eisner acts like he's forgotten, then says, "I almost got away with it." He reports that the preliminary count shows 43 percent withheld their votes.[1] The shareholders have spoken. Now it's up to the board to determine Eisner's fate.

And it's up to me, and the few other famished investors still here, to find something nutritious to eat.

A few hours later at a Disney board meeting, Eisner steps down as chairman but retains, for the moment, his CEO title. His undoing was at least partly due to his imperial attitude. There's a lesson in that. The next CEO I encounter makes it a point to shake the hand of every investor he can.

---

1. The final tally was over 45 percent.

In a nutshell . . .

DISNEY

EDUCATIONAL VALUE: A
  Endless Disney facts—way too many.
ENTERTAINMENT VALUE: A
  Human drama, TV/movie clips.
FREEBIES: F
  No free theme park passes since 1997.
FOOD & DRINK: F
  All-day meeting. No food. Starve 'em out!

INSIGHT: Shareholder democracy is a nice concept, but sometimes there's no such thing. There's almost never any competition for board seats—the number of people nominated usually coordinates precisely with the number of openings—and it isn't possible to vote "no." Don't like a candidate? The best you can do is indicate that you "withhold" your vote. But if a lot of shareholders do that, it can send a powerful message.

13

Welcome to the Hotel Can'tAffordYa

DUPONT

Disclosure: When DuPont was founded in 1802, it made gunpowder. A century later it was a dynamite company—literally. I had heard that the legacy of those early days was that every DuPont meeting, no matter how small, still begins with a review of evacuation procedures just in case something goes terribly wrong. That sounded intriguing, but what led me to make a small investment was the desire to visit a shareholder meeting that was sure to be held at the DuPont Theatre, in the legendary and luxurious Hotel DuPont. Many venues for annual meetings are big, nondescript rooms filled with rows of dark gray folding metal chairs. At the Hotel DuPont there's no such thing as a nondescript room.

You could blink and miss Delaware. So how is it that this state—a mere one hundred miles long and thirty miles across—is the legal home for more than half of all the corporations listed on the New York Stock Exchange? Some say it's because Delaware is business-friendly, and others will tell you it's because the state's courts have more experience than most when it comes to corporate concerns. Both sides may well be saying the same thing. In any case, few would argue that relatively inexpensive corporate registration fees are also part of the reason.

Not all companies registered in Delaware hold their shareholder meetings in the state, but some of the nation's oldest and largest firms do. When they do, they almost always hold them at the Hotel DuPont, an astonishingly posh, old-style urban palace in the heart of otherwise bland Wilmington.

Usually when I'm attending a shareholder meeting, I save money by staying somewhere other than the hotel where the function is taking place. In this case, it's worth making an exception to try a night at a place that has hosted John F. Kennedy, Joe DiMaggio, and Katharine Hepburn, among other luminaries.

I convince my wife, Nancy, to take a day off and tag along to enjoy the fancy digs. At check-in, she's somewhat appalled to discover we're paying $319 ($350+, including taxes) for a single night in a standard room. We're both amused to be told that amount can be reduced by fifty cents if we can live without having a copy of *USA Today* delivered to our door in the morning.

A few minutes later we open the door to our tenth-floor corner room overlooking . . . well, downtown Wilmington. It's two or three times the size of a typical hotel room—as it probably ought to be, for the price. The ceilings are high and passageways arched. The walls are thick, although not enough to drown out the sounds of city buses on the street below. The bathroom is marble and there's a telephone next to the commode. You could land a helicopter on the bed. The walk-in closet is stocked with plush robes and slippers bearing the hotel's logo. There's a minibar stuffed with three-dollar Snickers, KitKats, and Pepsis.

On the table in the living room is a large volume called *The Ultimate Guide to Delaware*, and I can't help but wonder how such a tiny state (only Rhode Island is smaller) could merit such an impressive tome. The answer, I quickly discover, is that most of the pages are filled with advertising. Other neatly arranged reading materials include a variety of upper-end magazines and, not surprisingly, *DuPont* magazine, a collection of articles about products made by the DuPont company—which, of course, wouldn't dare hold its meeting anywhere else.

We're still exploring the room when there's a knock at the door. I open it and a snappily dressed bellhop holds out an envelope and asks, "Dr. Lazlo?" Suddenly I feel like I'm in a scene from *Casablanca*. Hmmm. I've never been mistaken for a *doctor* before. . . . Nah, it would be wrong, I decide.

The movie-set feeling lingers throughout our stay. Everyone's in costume—the employees in their smartly pressed uniforms and the guests who wouldn't feel comfortable wearing jeans in a place like this. Conversations are quiet and the language is formal. I'm called "sir" so often that I feel like I may have been knighted when I wasn't paying attention.

We go downstairs in the morning, figuring we'll have better luck finding an inexpensive breakfast at a nearby restaurant, and we're surprised to stumble into a complimentary buffet in the massive, gilded Green Room off the lobby. We're even more surprised when we learn that we've wandered into an unadvertised reception for DuPont shareholders. Silver trays loaded with miniature muffins don't seem very popular, but I grab one of each— raspberry, chocolate chip, banana, and blueberry. After one bite, I understand: they're made with a new soy product DuPont is pushing, and they taste a little odd.

Next to me, a couple in their early sixties seems to be thinking the same thing. We strike up a conversation and I find that we're kindred spirits. They've also been to a few shareholder meetings in recent years to learn more about "their" companies and figured they would see what this one was all about.

"We're retired. We'll go anywhere for a cup of coffee and a Danish," Shirley Pine jokes. It turns out her husband, Joe, has another reason for wanting to be here. "I was a driver for a big company," he tells me, "and on shareholder meeting day we were always told not to talk to the CEO. I never understood why that day was different, but I'm sure there's more stress on the guy who runs the show."

Somebody's sure uptight, judging from the intense security we go through when we walk down the hall to the DuPont Theatre, where the shareholder meeting will be held. First, I need to show my ID and a copy of my brokerage statement, to prove I'm a shareholder (although just barely: If my math is right, my 100 shares amount to one *millionth* of the 996,780,000 outstanding). Then there's a metal detector and a bag search. After that, another ID check. Finally I'm in.

The auditorium is the sort of highly civilized place anyone's Aunt Maude would write home about—red velvet ropes, gilded walls, sparkling chandeliers, six hundred or so cushy seats. According to signs in the lobby, *Riverdance* is being performed here each evening. This morning's headliner—DuPont's CEO and chairman, Chad Holliday—proves to be just as spirited as those in the Irish dancing extravaganza and has the added advantage of being able to use his arms. Before the meeting he wanders up and down the aisles, shaking hands with shareholders and showing political polish similar to Bill Clinton's. If he's stressed out, it doesn't show.

I'm awed until Shirley Pine, who's sitting next to me, puts things in perspective: "For the millions he makes, I'd shake everybody's hands, too!" (Holliday's $3.4 million total compensation in 2004 ranks 248th among CEOs of the nation's 500 largest companies, according to *Forbes*. By comparison, Warren Buffett's $100,000 ranks 488th. The CEO with the lowest paycheck of all is Richard Kinder, who heads an oil and gas pipeline outfit called Kinder Morgan: He works for $1 a year. The lower the paycheck, the more an executive's financial health depends on managing the company well enough to ensure that his or her shares pay healthy dividends and/or go up in value.)

Holliday's well-intentioned germ-spreading comes to a halt when a loud, fast-paced movie begins. DuPont makes hundreds of products, and we probably get to see most of them in the next three minutes as a dizzying array of images cascades across the screen—everything from kitchen counters to space vehicles. Suddenly it ends, with a child's whispered "The miracles of science!" whooshing through the speakers.

I'm impressed. But I'm eager to see how they'll tell us what to do if someone accidentally tosses a lit cigarette toward a TNT storage closet. A cartoon featuring Wile E. Coyote and the Roadrunner might do the job quite nicely, I think. No such luck. A voice over the PA system intones a vague and humorless: "Please take a moment to acquaint yourselves with the exits, in the event we have to evacuate the building."

With no further ado, there's another movie. This one is less MTV and more Spielberg. Beautifully lit scenes illustrating "leaps of faith"—clean water and lifesaving medicines among them—are accompanied by a majestic soundtrack, which soars to a crescendo as the words "The people of DuPont have taken leaps" fill the screen. It's inspiring, and I join in the applause.

CEO Holliday takes advantage of the moment to bound onto the stage like a talk-show host, himself clapping all the while. He greets us with a booming "Good morning!" and starts to tell us what DuPont's been up to lately.

He reminds me of a preacher (or a Wal-Mart executive) as he strolls around and tells us in no uncertain terms and a distinct Southern accent that DuPont is "the mos' dynamic science company in the whirl." There's an obligatory reference to the company's long history, followed—ironically, I think—by an invocation of "Six Sigma," a trendy management concept that has something to do with trying to achieve near perfection as gauged by standard deviations— whatever *those* are. (They sound like measures of average behavior by unusual people, or perhaps vice versa.)

To hear Holliday tell it, Six Sigma involves "people working directly in the workplace on process improvement." I've heard any number of executives talk about Six Sigma, and no two have ever defined it in the same way, so I've filed the term under "suspected crapola" and generally avoided investing in any companies where it's held sacred. (As always, your mileage may vary.)

Apparently, Six Sigmas may not be enough, because Holliday is admitting, "We're not satisfied with our stock performance." There hasn't been much to be happy about. The stock price as of April 2004 is right around where it was six years earlier.

"The goal is zero," says Holliday. That would be alarming if he were still talking about the stock price, but he's moved on to "core values"—ideas such as eliminating pollution and on-the-job injuries.

Seconds later Holliday is recognizing groups of DuPont employees for achievements like "record growth in ethylene copolymers," and I realize I have no idea what ethylene copolymers are—a clear violation of my self-imposed know-what-you-own rule, which may need a bit of tweaking. Aw, heck, you can't know everything. Or maybe you can: Next, Holliday lauds another group of employees for improving safety in a convenience store chain, declaring, "Twenty-three hundred injuries have been avoided in WaWa stores." How could anyone know *that?* ("See the woman over in the beverages aisle? She just opened and closed a freezer door without hurting herself. Chalk up another injury averted! Wait, she's left the store without slipping and falling—that's *two!*")

There are three shareholder proposals listed on the agenda, and each seems to have potential to spark some lively debate. That's probably why the program distributed at the door specifies that speakers will be limited to two minutes each, and that "personal matters, grievances or litigation, and specific collective bargaining issues, are not appropriate for this meeting."

The first of those rules, at least, seems almost sure to be broken. Gadfly Evelyn Davis is scheduled to propose that DuPont produce an annual list of all company associates who have worked for the government in the past five years and might have in some way influenced DuPont contracts. But Holliday tells us that Davis isn't present, so he's promised her that he will introduce her proposal. He quickly refers us to the written presentation in the proxy statement and considers his job done. Davis's reputation precedes her. Some in the audience are relieved while others are disappointed by her absence.

The second proposal seeks a company-wide human rights policy permitting all workers to join unions. Earlier, I had looked outside the front entrance of the hotel to see if there were any protesters (or if anyone was dumping

150 pounds of "pollution" at the door, as environmental activists tried to do at AK Steel's 2002 shareholder meeting). Sure enough, there had been about a dozen union members pacing the sidewalk while politely handing out fliers outlining the proposal and suggesting that DuPont's cozy relationships with various government officials around the world were endangering workers' rights. Here inside the meeting, their proposal is made by a union spokesman who has been with DuPont for twenty years. Unfortunately, he reads the words as though it's the first time he's ever seen them, and the crowd begins to fidget. No matter how noble the cause, if you want people to be on your side, you can't bore 'em.

Luckily, a much more animated union rep delivers the third proposal, seeking tighter limits on executive compensation at DuPont. He says that at each of the past six shareholder meetings, Holliday has talked about how the company is "turning the corner," yet the stock price has fallen over the period. Meanwhile, the CEO has been granted options to buy more than three million shares. "If the stock simply goes back to where it was when Holliday became the CEO (in February 1998), his options will be worth $90 million while shareholders haven't made a dime," the spokesman says, picking up steam as he speaks. "Poor performance should not be rewarded! What's expected of our employees should be expected of our CEO. Stop the financial madness. Enough is enough!"

His rant sets the tone for the Q&A, which seems to consist almost entirely of material that whoever wrote the "meeting procedures" in the program hoped to ban. First, a series of DuPont retirees come to the microphones, and each takes a piece of Holliday. Several criticize DuPont's purchase of oil giant Conoco in 1981 (a $7.4 billion deal—the largest in history, at that point) and subsequent spin-off eighteen years later. One invokes the Conoco transactions and the $4.2 billion sale, announced today, of a fibers division: "I've heard you say some of your acquisitions didn't fit. Some of your decisions *give* me fits! I don't want to see that $4.2 billion get sucked up by you getting bonuses."

The elderly widow of a DuPont retiree stands and says the company has been shrinking the survivor's pension benefits she's been receiving since 1986. It's currently at $116 a month, she says, adding angrily that she's "shocked by how DuPont treats its former employees and their survivors. It's a disgrace."

Holliday—who until now has been merely thanking people for their comments—counters, "Most companies don't offer survivor benefits. We're trying to keep health benefits up."

A union rep disagrees: "I'd like to enlighten you a little bit about survivor benefits. Other big companies have them. You need to get out of the DuPont Building and look around. The company's view seems to be, 'We know we might give you cancer, but we're certainly going to limit our liability once you have it.'"

Holliday's answer was surely scripted earlier by a lawyer, somewhere. "We have never knowingly used a process or a product that was unsafe for our people."

The union rep explodes. "We're exposed to *chemicals!* We're not working in *cookie factories!*"

No sooner has that fire died down than another one erupts. A senior citizen in the front row says he doesn't like it that the proxy statement mentions that one of DuPont's directors is also a director at Planned Parenthood. The man calls it "the organization that promotes baby abortions" and suggests the description should be removed because it implies DuPont's approval. Another shareholder takes issue, arguing that what the director does "with his own time doesn't interfere with the purpose and productivity of DuPont." The original speaker responds incredulously: "What he does on his own time shouldn't be part of DuPont's business? *When do you think life begins?*"

I'm still puzzling through how those two sentences could be related when a shareholder in the balcony changes the subject. He gives Holliday grief about letting jobs go overseas: "What about DuPont's commitment to the U.S.?" The CEO sidesteps the employment issue and says his focus is on competing globally.

When Holliday says there's time for just one more question, cordiality returns. The shareholder who had railed against abortion steps up and thanks the staff and Holliday for their courtesy, then adds, "I just wish I could do a better job of convincing you I'm right." It's a nice gesture, but it occurs to me that he's used a pretext—one director's work for a charity—to preach his own version of the gospel, and that's sort of annoying. I wonder how he would feel if he were at GE's shareholder meeting and someone with an opposite view nattered on about potential interpretations of that company's old slogan, "We bring good things to life."

A closing film takes us through a rapid history of the company, synthesizer music swelling as the camera zooms on still images, and then the show's over. It seems to take an extraordinarily long time for the audience to move through the exit to the lobby—long enough that I'm glad we didn't have to put the evacuation drill to a test. I speculate that maybe they're sending all of us home with slabs of Corian— a DuPont product—that we can use to renovate our kitchen counters, and people are having trouble hauling the stuff away. As it turns out, the delay is caused by Holliday himself. He's a one-man receiving line at the exit, shaking every hand—in some cases for the second or third time.

In the lobby, I say good-bye to Shirley and Joe Pine. They're headed over to Atlantic City to visit a casino or two and see if investing some quarters in slot machines might pay off better than their investment in DuPont has recently. Me, I'm headed for Las Vegas to do pretty much the same thing.

In a nutshell . . .
DuPont

EDUCATIONAL VALUE: **A**
Solid overview.

ENTERTAINMENT VALUE: **A**
Several films, gregarious CEO.

FREEBIES: **F**
None.

FOOD & DRINK: **C**
Breakfast buffet featuring company's soy products.

INSIGHT: The historic Hotel DuPont is a favored shareholder meeting location for many older, well-established companies. Small wonder. It's in a state generally regarded as business-friendly, and it caters perfectly to the old-money crowd.

14

You Bettor, You Bet

MGM MIRAGE

Disclosure: I'm not much of a gambler, but at 2:30 in the morning one day in late 1985, I won sixteen hundred dollars on a single pull of a slot machine at a Las Vegas casino. I figure that means over my lifetime I've at least broken even on such ventures. When I decided it would be interesting to buy a few shares in a "gaming" company (the term Wall Street uses to avoid any association with gambling), MGM Mirage seemed most attractive in several ways—not least because it includes most of the poshest properties on the Strip.

All investments are gambles, to some extent. So owning a piece of the casinos would seem to be a nice way to hedge your bet.

At least that's what I'm telling myself as I stroll among the slot machines at New York–New York in Las Vegas, heading for MGM Mirage's 2004 shareholder meeting. It's early, but the players are here. Lights are flashing, and it almost sounds like more coins are coming out than are going in. Almost.

There's a parade of greeters on the job, making sure shareholders find the way to the Zumanity Theater, normally home to Cirque du Soleil, the resident circus troupe for whom the venue was built. I already know the slalom route through the distractions, because I scoped out the meeting location the night before. In the process, I marveled at how effectively the casino's designers had captured details of Manhattan. The "streets" even include manhole covers with steam rising from them.

The box office outside the theater is already open, selling tickets for two *Zumanity* shows this evening—one at 8:00 and one at 11:00—that I'm relatively confident won't bear much resemblance to what will take place in the theater this morning. Oh, there may be a little song and dance in both cases (figuratively this morning and literally this evening), but that's where any similarities will end, I imagine. Still, there's only one way to be sure. On a whim, I buy a ticket to the 8:00 show. Alas, there's no shareholder discount.

After the registration table, there's a big breakfast spread. I grab a pastry and a cup of Starbucks coffee—*I'm weakening!*—and head inside the theater. It's every bit as ornate as the DuPont Theatre but without the "old money" feel. A huge stage is washed with dramatic red lighting and flanked by spiral staircases. Right away I notice how quiet the room is. I also notice a rose petal or two falling from the ceiling. Now *there's* a classy way to make the investors feel welcome. I figure they're probably strays from last night's show.

There's an odd little island down in the middle of what's almost certainly the center ring when the circus is in the house. Atop the island is a table with five chairs behind it. On a large screen at the front of the room there's a slide of the company's logo. At the tick of 10:00 a.m., the screen comes to life with a slick music video presentation of the company's properties here in Nevada (where it has ten casinos in all and is the state's largest employer) as well as in Atlantic City, Detroit, and Biloxi.

Meanwhile, I'm counting heads and am surprised by the low turnout—maybe fifty people in all, more than a few wearing Bermuda shorts. But suddenly a side door opens, and the number of people present doubles as a long stream of men in dark suits files in and installs itself in the front of the room. One of the men looks familiar, but I can't quite place him.

MGM's CEO, Terry Lanni, who looks a bit like Hubert Humphrey, gets things started by apologizing on behalf of Kirk Kerkorian, the octogenarian jillionaire who is the company's largest shareholder and serves as a director. Kerkorian isn't able to join us today, because he's renovating Spain, or something like that. When Lanni introduces the other directors, I realize why one face looked familiar a minute ago: General Alexander Haig is on the board. Haig served as President Ronald Reagan's secretary of state and famously announced that he was in charge at the White House when Reagan was shot. I'm relieved to know that if Lanni suddenly keels over, Haig's here.

Fortunately, Lanni's doing just fine. He's a confident but not aggressive speaker, who prides himself on not fitting the flashy stereotype for a casino boss; in fact, he lives in Pasadena, California—more than two hundred miles west—and only spends three days a week in Las Vegas.

He wastes no time getting through a wrap-up of the past year. In a word, he seems "Focused." Coincidentally, that very word is on the front of the 2004 annual report, reproduced on the screen behind Lanni.

He tells us that MGM Mirage's long-term vision is "maximizing the profit potential of our undeveloped land" and observes that the company owns more prime real estate in Las Vegas and in Atlantic City than anyone else. He introduces a short film about Borgata, the company's Atlantic City showplace; it leaves the impression that everyone arrives at the place riding a Vespa, which seems unlikely. He dangles the possibility of MGM casinos in the United Kingdom, Macau (just off the coast of China), and on Sentosa Island (just off the coast of Singapore—and coincidentally, already home to a dancing waters show and a wishing well where people tend to dispose of coins in hopes of pleasant paybacks). He says all the right things about having a diversified workforce and adds that *Fortune* magazine has cited the company's success in that area. Finally, Lanni asks for the preliminary results of the voting to "see if we'll be around here next year" and brings the official business meeting to a very efficient end just a half hour after it began.

He's just as impressive when handling the Q&A that follows. One of the impressive characteristics about Warren Buffett is that he can and does cite, from memory, all sorts of data. Lanni seems to have a similar gift. When a shareholder asks a vague question about the possibility of MGM developing a relationship with a racetrack in New York, Lanni knows the exact dollar amount concerned and the precise details of the legislation that might help make it happen.

Another shareholder wonders about the prospects for a high-speed train between Las Vegas and the Los Angeles area, which would make it possible for money from Southern Californians to spend more time in Nevada. Lanni explains that government funding for that project isn't currently available, but he thinks it will happen, eventually. A third shareholder asks the inevitable question at shareholder meetings of companies that don't pay dividends: Why not? Lanni's answer is equally predictable: the board discusses the idea regularly but feels that reinvesting earnings in the business is more desirable.

As the Q&A winds down, I could swear I hear a random musical note or two from backstage. Sure enough, there's a special treat for shareholders. Two *Zumanity* performers, Olga and Alan, are on hand to entertain. A band plays New Orleans–style blues from a catwalk over the stage. As a fat trumpet wails, tall, blonde Olga and Alan, her muscular dwarf admirer, fly around the stage, using oversize scarves like Rapunzel's hair. Their airborne acrobatics describe attraction, rejection, love, and sex.

Ten or so hours later—this time with a drink stronger than coffee in my hand—I watch the same scene all over again. I note a key difference: During the morning performance, you couldn't see right through Olga's top. Hinting at sex is okay in a shareholder meeting, but at sixty-five dollars a ticket you've got to deliver the goods. *This* show begins with a "Puritan" shouting, "Do you want to see tits?" and ends with cast members and a few folks from the audience piling onto each other in a simulated orgy, egged on by a transvestite master of ceremonies. What a difference a few hours makes!

No trip to Las Vegas would be complete without putting a quarter or two in a machine and pulling the lever (or pushing the button) to see what happens. So, strictly in the name of research, Nancy and I hopscotch up and down the Strip—despite a howling dust storm—stopping at each of MGM Mirage's seven properties to play precisely ten dollars (half in quarters and half in dollar coins). I'm wondering if my luck is still any good in this town.

First up is Bellagio, a high-class joint by any measure.

Out front there's a spectacular eight-and-a-half acre lake—in the middle of the desert!—where nearly five thousand lights and two hundred-plus loudspeakers are engaged every few minutes in a dancing waters show, featuring fountains soaring 250 feet high in synch with songs everyone knows. Inside, the lobby smells of flowers, not cigarette smoke, thanks to a huge, beautifully mani-cured conservatory filled with roses. There's also an art gallery featuring original works by Monet, and there's a $25.00 per person lunch buffet that's worth the price. I figure that the slot payoffs in a place like this are bound to be a bit less generous because the other attractions are more than ample, but when I'm through feeding $10.00 to the slot machines I'm pleased to discover that $9.85 has come back to me. Fifteen cents to enjoy Bel-lagio? You bet.

Next we stop by the monstrous, emerald-lit and Oz-themed MGM Grand Hotel, where we're staying. Our room is one of more than five thousand—and based on the walk to it from the registration desk, it may well actually be in Kansas. There's a little bit of everything at this flagship property—a Rain Forest Café filled with shrieking chil-dren, a glassed-in area that's home to some suspiciously docile lions, a Studio 54 nightclub for suspiciously-energetic-in-the-wee-hours humans, and even a "test screening" facility used by TV networks to get an early read on pilot programs. (In exchange for a twenty-dollar gift certificate redeemable only at a TV-show-themed store where virtually everything costs at least twenty dollars more than it should, we get suckered into spending an hour watching an abomination in which ne'er-do-well graffiti taggers are supposed to be sympathetic characters. I'm hopeful that our reactions help save the American public from ever having this horror turn up on a network schedule.) When we checked in, we were handed a book of two-for-one coupons for use in the hotel. Unfortunately, that equation works in reverse when I feed my ten dollars into the MGM Grand Hotel's slot machines. The house keeps half.

Our third stop is the Mirage, where a volcano out front erupts every fifteen minutes. Just a decade or so before, the Mirage had been as good as it gets in Las Vegas. It's still a fabulous place with a lush lobby featuring a tropical fish tank that must be a hundred feet long, but the spirit's gone. The area where Siegfried and Roy's white tigers lived is empty and dark, just a few months after one of the big cats had taken a chunk out of Roy and the long-running show came to an abrupt end. I'm not complaining, though, because here my $10.00 turns into $11.25. So far I've "invested" $30.00 and I'm down by $3.90.

TI is the flirtatious next-door neighbor to the Mirage. Formerly known as Treasure Island and for regular full-scale pirate ship battles in the lagoon out front, facing the Strip, TI is now pushing T&A. Apparently the ships have new crews—dancing cheerleader types called Sirens, whose images adorn calendars, mouse pads, and T-shirts in the hotel's gift shop. I don't buy any—or, alas, even catch their act—because I'm on a mission. So is TI, apparently, because in no time at all my ten dollars turns into a mere seventy-five cents. Ouch.

We return to New York–New York, the casino that hosted the shareholder meeting earlier in the day and the Cirque du Soleil show earlier in the evening. Perhaps if I can make it here, I can make it anywhere. On the other hand, I've seldom left the real New York with much money left in my pocket. Amazingly, ten dollars here becomes thirteen dollars.

The two casinos left on the list are the Boardwalk and Monte Carlo, modest entries on the Strip whose current functions are probably to keep the real estate occupied and profitable while MGM's executives look at grander schemes. At Boardwalk I'm shut out completely for the first time. Every coin I put in the slot stays put, and of the $60.00 total I've played so far, only $39.85 remains. My "investment" is down by more than a third. If it were a stock and I hadn't already gotten out by now, I would have to feel very strongly that I knew more than the average bear (or bull) about what would happen next.

What does happen next is a very pleasant surprise. Nearly every time I spin the wheels at Monte Carlo, they stop in a neat row of matching fruit icons and there's a welcome rattle in the coin tray below. In mere minutes my final $10.00 has grown to $33.00—so the $70.00 I had set out with has become $72.85. Now, a $2.85 gain over four hours may not seem like much. But it works out to a gain of $17.10 a day, or $6,214.50 a year. Of course, what are the odds this wasn't a fluke? Not very good, I'd say. All in all, I think I'll be better off owning the stock and making money when other people choose to bet.

My miniature windfall is about to come in handy. There's an admission charge for the next meeting on my itinerary.

In a nutshell . . .

MGM Mirage

EDUCATIONAL VALUE: B
   Walking through the casino spoke volumes.
ENTERTAINMENT VALUE: A
   Cirque du Soleil!
FREEBIES: F
   None.
FOOD & DRINK: B
   Coffee, heaps of pastries.

INSIGHT: Sometimes the location of a shareholder meeting enables you to take a tour of the plant, as it were. Of course, official plant tours will focus only on what the company's managers want you to see. Opportunities for self-guided tours are rare and usually lack the play-by-play, but wandering the facilities on your own can provide a rewarding look at your company.

15

Life Is a Cabernet
CHALONE WINE GROUP

Disclosure: The same cousin who suggested that Playboy's shareholder meeting might be worth a look told me about Chalone Wine Group, and his logic was the same—sounds like fun! In both cases, I bought one hundred shares just to be able to attend. (It can be tricky to do that, because you need to own shares as of the "record date" set by the company's board—and they don't announce it in advance. To be on the safe side, think in terms of buying within nine months of the previous shareholder meeting.)

Can a company get away with holding its annual meeting high atop a remote California mountain (140 miles south of San Francisco and 277 miles north of Los Angeles), on a Saturday, and charging shareholders ninety dollars each to attend? Throw in the tab for a hotel in not-so-nearby Monterey or Carmel and it makes for a pricey event.

You'd be hard-pressed to find any Chalone Wine Group shareholders who feel it isn't worth the inconvenience and the expense to be present. In fact, most of the thirteen hundred or so people here will readily admit they own shares in the company simply so they can be assured of being invited. There aren't many companies where the main attraction for investors is the shareholder meeting itself, but this is one where few shareholders care if the stock price goes up or down.

Technically, this isn't really the official shareholder meeting at all. This is the 2004 "shareholder celebration"— a high-class outdoor feast where the company's products flow freely. It was decoupled from the official business meeting a few years ago. As a shareholder, I could have attended either, or both. Something tells me this gathering will be more fun and perhaps just as educational. Besides, Nancy is willing to join me for a "celebration" much more readily than for a business meeting.

We're heading south on I-5, just past Salinas—a sleepy agricultural hamlet featuring a terrific museum commemorating native son John Steinbeck—when we pass Soledad Prison, a gloomy-looking maximum security facility, just before the turnoff for the winery. It's a sobering reminder that at least one of us shouldn't have too much wine today.

The vineyard is still a long drive up a bumpy one-lane mountain road, with switchbacks. At the top, we park in a huge just-mowed parking area scarred with more holes than a Buffalo byway in springtime. A happy young man in a golf cart pulls up and offers us a ride to the entrance. He's wearing a Hawaiian shirt, which means either that I've chosen appropriate clothing for the event or that, later on, people will think I'm the guy with the golf cart and hit me up for rides to their cars. When I ask him if he was hired for the occasion, he laughs and fesses up to being the company's comptroller—the guy in charge of balancing the books. "I got deputized for the day," he says. We thump through one of the holes, and he tells me that they were dug by badgers. "A lot of 'em up here," he explains. What he doesn't say is that badgers like to eat rodents, so there are probably a few of them around, too—and where there are rodents, in these parts, there also tend to be rattlesnakes. Fortunately, badgers eat them, too.

Wildlife sightings begin immediately. Even before we arrive at the gate we've spotted a big ape. It's an inflatable King Kong, underscoring the soirée's "Hollywood and Vine" theme.

As we sign in, we're handed souvenir glasses prefilled with champagne and some nifty little snack trays with notches to tuck the glasses into so you can carry the whole shebang with one hand. If there's a better way to welcome guests at a celebration, I don't know what it is.

The site is dominated by a white tent nearly the size of a football field. Under it is a sea of tables and chairs with a stage in the middle occupied by a band, the Martini Brothers, whose vocalist is channeling Sinatra. Scattered around the tent are tables loaded with cheeses, bread, and oysters, and many shareholders are testing the limits of their snack trays. There's also a popcorn wagon and even a table where you can grab a fistful of animal crackers and dip them in chocolate sauce.

Each of Chalone's dozen wine labels—Acacia, Canoe Ridge, Chateau Duhart-Milon, Dynamite, Echelon, Edna Valley, Hewitt, Jade Mountain, Moon Mountain, Orogeny, Provenance, and Sagelands—has a booth of its own, all more than happy to offer tastes. My lovely wife generously observes that we're here in the name of research, so I should feel free to do whatever seems necessary. In other words, she'll see to it we get back to Monterey safely.

Many of the tasting stations feature carnival games

designed to produce winners more often than not, even if
the contestants have been drinking. At the Moon Mountain booth, I somehow hit the side of a barn with a dart
and am awarded a choice of hideous oversized goggles or
a hideous spangled bow tie. I choose the latter and don it
with pride. Throughout the day, there's a knowing nod
whenever I run into anyone similarly attired. My collection of prizes and freebies eventually includes a model airplane kit (courtesy of King Kong's assistant), a set of
coasters, and a miniature bottle of Provenance's Cabernet
Sauvignon in a five-inch wooden case.

The most crowded booth is the one where shareholders—
and their guests for the day—can place wine orders at
major discounts, with free shipping on purchases over
$250. There's a long line of people paying anything from
$8 for a bottle of simple Chardonnay to nearly $500 for a
whopping six-liter bottle of Hewitt's 2001 Cabernet
Sauvignon.

Nearly as popular is the silent auction tent, where shareholders can bid on bottles and B&B stays, among other
things. The proceeds will go to the Woodward/Graff Wine
Foundation—a nonprofit organization set up by Chalone's
founders that provides scholarships to "deserving students
of the art and science of wine, food and hospitality." In
other words, a cause that everyone here would surely agree
is worthy.

Groucho and Marilyn imitators are busy working the
crowd when a voice over the loudspeaker beckons us to
our seats inside the big top. We're the only first-timers
at our table, and the experience of our new comrades
proves valuable right off the bat. Dozens of servers are
ensuring that the eight people at each table have no
fewer than four bottles of wine to enjoy; when they reach

our table, the old hands somehow convince them that we merit two additional bottles.

The fiftyish man sitting next to me is filling out a wine order with the urgency of a mathematician on the verge of solving a complex equation. When he's finished, he turns and introduces the woman with him as "DD." I figure that's her name until he explains, a few seconds later, that he means "Designated Driver." He's Bob Jarvis, a political science professor from Santa Cruz. Everyone at the table except us turns out to be from California.

Chalone's president, Tom Selfridge, greets the crowd and makes it clear that my wife and I aren't the only "foreigners" atop the mountain today: Forty-one states and seven countries are represented. He explains that this is the thirty-fifth such gathering. The first, held in a kitchen, drew six people and was over in ten minutes—not counting a few hours of wine drinking afterward. Word apparently spread quickly, because two years later there were fifty attendees, and by 1986 more than five hundred shareholders and guests showed up. Selfridge points out that this gathering draws a much bigger crowd than shareholder meetings for many Fortune 500 companies.

As he's talking, the servers deliver antipasto trays brimming with focaccia, artichokes, sausages, salami, and grilled asparagus.

In keeping with the everyone-wins-a-prize spirit of the day, Selfridge presents "Academy Awards" to representatives for each of the Chalone labels. During the ceremony, I notice that our table's wine supply seems to be disappearing rapidly. Bob notices, too—and he's quick to point a finger at Ed, a curly-haired gent on the other side of the table who has apparently taken to sharing our good fortune with thirsty people outside our group. Ed's sheepish but promises to make it up to us by finagling replacement bottles, and he's as good as his word.

Selfridge closes by announcing that we should all check under our chairs, because one person seated at each table will find an envelope containing a certificate good for a free bottle of wine. "DD" shrieks victoriously, and I realize I probably used up my luck during that casino crawl in Nevada a few days earlier.

The remarkable buffet is all the more amazing when one considers that the caterers had to bring it up the same road we took. Entrees include chicken with lemon, roast salmon on couscous, and sirloin with garlic, soy, and ginger. There's a baby spinach salad, a Yukon potato salad, a roasted beet salad, a white bean salad with lobster, and a bean salad with black truffle vinaigrette. And there are bread and cheese tables also jammed with figs, grapes, apricots, and pecans. Even for a vegetarian like me it's a feast, capped with spectacular strawberry shortcake and washed down with yet more wine.

It's worth every penny. Free lunches at shareholder meetings are almost as elusive as the adage would indicate, anyway. In addition to Otter Tail's, I've encountered just two others so far.

I had never heard of Fulton Financial—a regional bank based in central Pennsylvania—but the name kept coming up when I asked people which shareholder meeting they liked best. Most seemed to be salivating as they told me about it. Couples looked at each other gooey-eyed and said, "Remember that chocolate cake?" In April 2003 I joined thousands of Fulton fans in the main hall of the Hershey Lodge and Convention Center, all with forks at the ready. The meal wasn't bad at all, and the chocolate-cocoa cake served for dessert was extraordinary indeed. Other than that, Fulton's meeting was run-of-the-mill.

American Italian Pasta, in Kansas City, invites its owners to belly up to a gourmet pasta bar after the shareholder meeting. There were about three hundred people at the 2004 gathering, many of them employees. I shared a table with a group of women who had been working night and day to develop low-carb pasta. We sat through the votes and the reports and some colorful presentations, including a "Sorry, but the pictures don't really do it justice" slide show by an employee who had won a trip to Italy for an idea that saved the company $250,000 a year. Finally, it was time for lunch. I'd been looking forward to it, figuring the odds were at least fair there would be something suitable for a vegetarian. Nope. There were five toppings: sausage, salmon, shrimp, beef, and chicken. So a few hours later I stuffed my face with cheese nachos at the airport. While I was munching, a group of bored businesspeople at the table next to me couldn't find a deck of cards and came up with an ingenious solution, asking the waitress for fifty-two napkins and a pen.

Here at the Chalone celebration, the fun and games are winding down. A handful of shareholders are dancing to the band's dead-on rendition of "Summer Wind" and several others—oblivious to the music and sated by food and drink—are napping (fewer, though, than I've seen at several other shareholder gatherings!). Most are slowly working their way to the parking lot, grabbing bottles of water from the ice buckets that Chalone has thoughtfully placed near the exit.

It's been a perfect day for wine lovers, many of whom are already talking about attending next year, when the theme would be "Vino Las Vegas."

Little do any of us know that just two days later there will be news that the party may be over forever. Chalone has long had a partnership with Domaines des Barons de Rothschild. The French group makes Chateau Duhart-Milon wine, one of Chalone's most respected labels. It also owns nearly half of Chalone's stock. Now it wants to buy the rest, and it has joined with two partners to do just that. Announcements like this can often be good news for existing shareholders, because the buyers typically pay a handsome premium over the stock price. Sometimes the activity attracts a competing bidder who is willing to pay even more.

Sure enough, the stock price begins to rise. But I'm wary. One of Rothschild's partners is Constellation Brands, a rapidly growing wine distributor that will be the world's largest just a year or so later. Constellation was once Canandaigua Brands, known for producing Wild Irish Rose. It still sells the low-rent stuff but has rounded out its offerings, and the Chalone labels would add more prestige.

As it happens, I had attended Constellation's shareholder meeting in Rochester, New York, in July 2002, and had come away somewhat underwhelmed (although not enough to sell my shares). The CEO/chairman/president, Richard Sands, insisted that a much-reported wine glut didn't exist—and that even if it did, his company wasn't affected, because there was only too much *inexpensive* wine (such as Wild Irish Rose?). An endless "rock video" takeoff on Billy Joel's "We Didn't Start the Fire," revamped as "We Really Lit the Fire," featured tortured lyrics praising synergies and stock splits. Worst of all was a very bizarre slide that went entirely unexplained, as near as I could tell. Picture this:

"Constellation Brands" in the center . . . an arrow pointing left to "Strategy" . . . an arrow pointing right to "Maximizing shareholder value" . . . an arrow pointing down to "Linkages" . . . and arrows pointing left and right from "Linkages" to "Division" and "Planning." I'm not sure where the x representing the quarterback was. To Constellation's credit, it gave attendees a small bottle of decent wine—and investors in the stock have had little cause to complain.

The Rothschild consortium's bid for Chalone is trumped by Diageo North America, the U.S. subsidiary of the British company that's the world's largest spirits distributor. Those of us who had bought Chalone stock during the past few years for $9.00 or so are pretty happy with the $14.25 Diageo pays for our shares—plus a one-time $1.00 per share "wine discount." Best of all, though, is one of the other terms of the deal: Diageo agrees to keep the annual celebrations going for another fifteen years.

If Chalone's meeting is so popular despite the remote location, the steep admission price, and the relative obscurity of the company itself, you might think that a much better known California firm—one with tens of thousands of rabid fans—could draw a decent crowd with a free gathering in a tourist Mecca. You'd be wrong, as I'm about to discover.

In a nutshell . . .

CHALONE WINE GROUP

EDUCATIONAL VALUE: **C**
    Learned a little about wine.
ENTERTAINMENT VALUE: **A**
    Carnival games, terrific band, silent auction, etc.
FREEBIES: **B**
    Commemorative wine glass/tray, game prizes.
FOOD & DRINK: **A+**
    Spectacular meal, plenty of fine wine.

INSIGHT: One of the ways companies express how they feel about their shareholders is through perks. Some offer discounts on company products. Others distribute goodie bags at shareholder meetings. A few are known for serving a free lunch. Rarest of all, perhaps, are those who raise a glass with their owners.

16

Sittin' on the Dock with eBay

EBAY

Disclosure: Over the past few years, I've bought quite a few HO-scale train cars through online auction powerhouse eBay. In several instances I've later discovered that the very same items were available in stores for less than the amounts of my winning bids. That's what I get for not doing my homework and determining reasonable prices in advance—probably a lesson better learned when buying toys than when investing in stocks! My shares in eBay—all five of 'em, hardly worth the time and trouble to sell—came from an investment I had made long ago through a limited partnership run by a venture capital firm that, luckily for me, did the homework.

Sometimes companies seem to play hide-and-seek with the annual meeting. You would think that Disney, for instance, would hold its event in Anaheim or Orlando, yet between 2002 and 2005 the company convened in Hartford, Denver, Philadelphia, and Minneapolis before finally coming home to Anaheim in 2006.

PetSmart, based in Phoenix, held its 2004 and 2005 meetings at the Four Seasons Hotel in Boston—apparently a convenient location for several of the company's directors but one that attracted only a handful of shareholders, me among them, in 2005. (Over the past decade, PetSmart's annual meeting has also been held in Dallas, Chicago, and New York, but not in Phoenix.)

Fred's, a discount retailer in the southern United States, has held all of its shareholder meetings since 2003 in Dublin, Georgia, which is nearly 140 miles from Atlanta and considerably farther than that from the company's headquarters in Memphis. Fred's does have a legitimate presence in Dublin, where it opened a distribution center in 2003. But it opened that facility after employees at its Memphis distribution center voted to unionize, and the union's spokesman has since taunted that Fred's holds its meetings at night because it "doesn't want any sun to shine on its actions." That's a bit of a stretch, considering that the sun's still quite visible in Georgia at dinnertime in mid-June, when Fred's convenes.

Some companies don't just take their meetings out into the country; they leave the country altogether. Morgan Stanley, for instance, held its 2002 gathering in London, while Tyco International held its meeting that year in Bermuda. (It works the other way, too. Canadian National Railway, based in Montreal, held its 2006 meeting in Memphis, which it called "a key operating centre on CN's North American rail network and an important destination for freight traffic." The company's CEO and president was born in Memphis.)

So what is eBay—based in San Jose—up to, convening its 2004 soirée in a New Orleans hotel, on the banks of the Mississippi?

And what's with the 8:00 a.m. start time? Few self-respecting visitors to this city call it a night before 2:00 a.m. If you want to discourage people from attending a function, one of the best ways to do it is to hold it early in the morning in a place like New Orleans (especially in the summer, when it's hot and sticky 24/7). Anyone who has never been to the Big Easy before is sure to be seduced by the nightlife and not very inclined (or rested enough) to take part in serious activities when the sun comes up.

I've been lucky enough to visit this wonderful city more or less once a year since 1990. The first visit was unforgettable. When I told a friend at the office that I was headed for New Orleans for a convention, she proudly told me she grew up there and promised to have one of her old classmates show me the town. Sure enough, a beautiful young woman met me when I arrived and took me on an amazing tour. "You'll discover the French Quarter all by yourself," she said, "so we're going to other places." And we did. We sipped drinks on the porch of The Columns (a funky mansion that served as the bordello where *Pretty Baby* was filmed), took a ride on the cranky but charming old streetcar that runs down the grassy strip in the middle of St. Charles Boulevard, and bowled at Mid-City Lanes while two terrific bands wailed on either side of us. We watched a parade of musicians, including a Neville Brother or two, perform at Tipitina's, a legendary club that's hosted anybody who's anybody. And we'd ended up at an astounding place called the F&M Patio Bar—an after-hours haunt where people were dancing on pool tables at three in the morning.

I don't think I got much out of my business meetings the next day. When I looked around me, I noticed that everyone else seemed to be in similar shape.

While I've managed to be more responsible on subsequent business visits, it's a struggle. There's great music everywhere you turn. Cold beer is just as ubiquitous, because it's legal to wander from watering hole to watering hole with a plastic "go-cup." And the food in New Orleans (home of famed chefs Paul Prudhomme and Emeril Lagasse) is so good that it's no wonder locals are among the roundest folks in all the land.

Last night I behaved myself. I had a quick beer at a Bourbon Street club around the corner from my French Quarter hotel and listened to blues chanteuse Marva Wright work her magic; then I called it a night while many tourists were just getting started. Still, it's hard to convince myself to head for a shareholder meeting rather than a cup of chicory coffee and a fresh beignet (a powdery pastry that must take two months or so to digest). It's almost as hard to find the meeting room itself. When I finally locate it, in an obscure corner of the Hilton, it's hard to believe that eBay is truly putting out the welcome mat.

That's confusing, because the town is crawling with eBay users. Just a few hours after the shareholder meeting, a three-day extravaganza called eBay Live! will open at the convention center. It will feature classes for buyers and sellers, two nicely catered receptions, loads of freebies from exhibitors, and even a wedding of two eBay community members. More than ten thousand people are registered for Live!

Yet here, in a relatively small, windowless room half a mile away, there are no more than a few dozen individual shareholders. We're nicely rewarded for our trouble: the logo hat, T-shirt, and notebook we get for free as we enter cost a pretty penny at the eBay Live! store, I later discover.

At a tiny head table sits Pierre Omidyar, who founded eBay in 1995. Omidyar is thirty-six but looks younger and sports a closely cropped mustache and beard. His ingenious creation—a global garage sale—has made him a billionaire. He focuses on philanthropy these days but continues to serve as eBay's chairman of the board, and he's in charge of this shareholder meeting. He looks a little nervous, like a man who would rather let someone else be the public face of his company. That someone else is Meg Whitman, the forty-seven-year-old president of eBay, who is standing nearby, wearing a navy pantsuit.

Omidyar quietly zips through the agenda. When he asks if shareholders have any comments, his eyes dart from left to right in search of raised hands—and finding none (it being so early in the morning and all), he offers a relieved "Great!" He's happy to get the votes on directors over as soon as possible and hand the spotlight over to Whitman.

She, on the other hand, is overjoyed to be here and to tell us all about how eBay's vision is "to provide a global online trading platform where practically anyone can trade practically anything." She's got statistics and she's not afraid to use them, so we learn:

- If eBay users were a country, that nation would be the eleventh most populous in the world (with 105 million inhabitants).

- More than four hundred thousand people make their living buying and selling things on eBay.

- Peak times are on Sunday morning, Sunday evening, and Monday evening, when the number of new listings ranges between three thousand to six thousand per *second*.

There's no reason to doubt that all of those statements are true, but if they are, then surely what Whitman says after that is a little unlikely: "We are at the earliest stages of building this company." Hmmm. Early on in my financial career, I had learned that it's wise to be wary of seemingly unstoppable growth. No tree grows to the sky, after all.

It's probably as good a time as any to pause for a few commercial messages, and that's what Whitman does, rolling three recent TV ads for eBay. The first features a guy who plans to use eBay to sell auto parts he hints might just be hot, and says the advantage of using eBay is that the buyers "will find me!" It ends with his wife looking forlorn and moaning, "Oh, no. Now he'll be home all the time!"

The second focuses on a Hong Kong toy car collector-turned-seller. He started the business in his bedroom and now has a four-thousand-square-foot facility, thanks to buying toy cars for twenty-nine Hong Kong dollars (about $3.77, U.S.) and selling them for twenty-nine U.S. dollars.

The third commercial tells the tale of a couple who run an art dealership in Arkansas. The husband exhorts the miracle of discovering that "Something here in Arkansas that ain't worth nothing to nobody is worth something to somebody somewhere else!" Like the first commercial, it ends with what passes for a joke about having to spend all day with a spouse.

While the last commercial rolls, a shaggy guy in his midthirties hurries into the room and sits in an empty chair next to me. Like several others in the small audience, he's wearing an eBay T-shirt and exuding hyperactivity. He might as well have "Type A" tattooed to his forehead.

Twitchy's hand shoots into the air as soon as the Q&A begins. He identifies himself as a "PowerSeller"—meaning he's probably among those who make their living via eBay deals—and asks Omidyar, "What's the real story behind eBay's start? Was it to sell Pez dispensers or to establish an effective marketplace?" Omidyar says the impetus of the marketplace was crucial, but he set out to help his wife (who was then his fiancée) to sell collectibles online—and wrote the initial program over a single weekend.

Another PowerSeller says she's eager to explore eBay Live! and suggests that next year the company might want to hold the event in Washington, D.C., to help legislators understand that online purchases should never be taxed. "Great idea!" Whitman responds, in the same enthusiastic tone Omidyar had used to express relief when there was no discussion of any issues up for a vote.

There aren't any hard questions. Indeed, there aren't many questions at all, and we're finished before 9:00 a.m. In the hallway on the way out, Whitman is talking about how her daughter has learned economics by trading Beanie Babies online.

I ask her why there are so few people here and she shrugs. "The shareholder meeting has never drawn much of a crowd." But with ten thousand eBay lovers in town—more than a few of whom probably own shares in the company—isn't this an opportunity to leverage your message? "That's why we hold it here with eBay Live! Tell your friends!" she says, cheerfully.

It's still hard to believe Whitman would have liked to see more faces at the meeting, considering that she presumably could have nixed the early start and the out-of-the-way location. But in fairness, shareholders who had come to New Orleans to see what eBay was all about could be forgiven for suspecting that Live! would be more educational (and entertaining) than the annual meeting.

I stroll through the soothing, air-conditioned Riverwalk shopping mall that stretches from the hotel to the massive (more than one million square feet) Ernest N. Morial Convention Center. It's swarming with people whose lives have been changed by eBay—a mix of puffy, bearded work-from-homers and hungry, young entrepreneurs with multiple cell phones hanging from their belts. At check-in I overhear a line that epitomizes the mind-set among attendees: "How much do you think that chandelier's worth?"

The planners at eBay have clearly done their homework. Lines move smoothly and events are well marked. Handouts for all the sessions have been collected on a CD-ROM given to all registrants. In the busiest "trade show" area I've ever seen, shippers, auction services, and financial companies are courting PowerSellers by inviting them to play games. Monster.com is sponsoring a "Build a Monster" race, for example, where participants pile up blocks to create a cardboard cretin. In each case, of course, the idea is to make sure everyone walks away with a prize—a stuffed animal, a ball, a shot glass—that has the sponsor's name on it.

Of course, the most conspicuous logo is eBay's. The company has set up a huge store right inside the entrance. Some of the items for sale don't surprise me at all—jackets, T-shirts, mugs, hats, packs, and water bottles. Others are more unusual, including eBay-emblazoned snow globes, Christmas tree ornaments, flip-flops, wrapping paper, digital cameras, commemorative coins, and even license plates reading "CUONEBAY." All in all, it puts the Microsoft "company store" to shame both in terms of imagination and audacity.

Still, the most coveted bit of logo merchandise in the place seems to be a thick plastic Earthlink glass. That's because it comes filled with a slushy local potion known as a hurricane—a mess of fruit juices and hard liquor (mostly rum), all red and sticky thanks to a splash of grenadine. On a hot day in New Orleans—and that's a redundant phrase in June—a hurricane (in a glass) is a wonderful thing.

It's a potion best washed down with a little food. Fortunately, there's more than a little on hand. The buffet for the opening night reception is arguably worth the price of admission to the entire conference (fifty to seventy dollars, depending on when you registered). It emphasizes local treats like mini-mufalettas (sandwiches stuffed with olive salad), Cajun chips, veggie crudités, and even tiny pecan pies. As I eat, a group of young Southern belles in Easter egg–colored plantation garb wanders past, giggling and greeting people at random. A few minutes later a jester and a bunch of other folks wearing Mardi Gras costumes romp through, tossing strings of plastic beads— some of which will surely be put to use later tonight on Bourbon Street, where adventuresome women often flash their breasts in exchange for the trinkets. Or so I've heard.

After pigging out on two or three desserts, I stumble into what seems to be an arts-and-crafts den in the middle of the exhibit hall. Construction paper, scissors, glue, glitter, and crayons are scattered across a series of tables. A few dozen people have pulled up chairs. Some are working industriously on the official mission—creating a giant wedding card for a couple who plan to tie the knot a few days later at this very conference. Others are simply enjoying having a place to sit, after downing a hurricane or two, and they look completely flummoxed by the idea of adding a message to a card for complete strangers.

During the rest of eBay Live! I'm surprised at myself for spending so much time in sessions at the convention center rather than goofing off in one of the best cities on the planet to goof off in. But a lot of the offerings are pretty hard for me to resist.

I'm intrigued by a session on "Writing Descriptions" for online auction items. The instructor is Griff—a bearded, roly-poly, high-energy, camp director–type in a baseball cap, T-shirt, and khakis. He was eBay's very first customer service rep, and he's learned a lot about what works and what doesn't in eBay listings. Stress rarity, he says. Don't use adjectives in the listing title; few people would include them in a search. For the same reason, don't use "Look!" in the title—even though thousands of listings do. If there are any flaws in the item you're selling, make sure they're highlighted in the description or accompanying photographs. And remember that humor can be a huge draw: an ad for a wedding gown, featuring a photo of it being worn by the guy who was left at the altar by his intended, drew more than seventeen million hits.

Griff is also at the helm for what turns out to be my favorite session, "Bizarre eBay Stories." Among the tales we hear over the next hour:

- The original site was called AuctionWeb, and it included a tab about the Ebola virus—a mysterious and deadly disease that breaks out periodically in Africa and gave Reston, Virginia, residents a scare in 1990 when a variation was found in lab animals there. (Omidyar was fascinated by the virus.)

- The company is called eBay because when Omidyar attempted to register his new venture in California as "Echo Bay," he discovered that name was already taken.

- Between 1996 and 1998, eBay's Web site crashed every hour.

- Griff discovered eBay early on and created a fictitious online identity for himself as "Uncle Griff," a fifty-something cross-dressing dairy farmer who lives with his dead-for-thirty-years mother and is a major proponent of duct tape. In character, he helped people figure out how to use eBay. Eventually the company noticed him and offered him a job. (Online identities are a big deal at eBay Live! because in many cases they're the only way these people know each other. So during Q&A sessions, it's not unusual for someone to stand up and introduce herself by saying, "Hi, I'm gorilla327 from Kansas"—and get applause from other attendees who recognize the user ID!)

■ The most expensive item ever listed was a Gulf-stream jet, for $4.9 million.

■ Someone once tried to sell "The Internet" for $1 million.

■ eBay won't allow listings for live animals, body parts, or things associated with gruesome tragedies—crumpled pieces of space shuttles, for example.

■ A man named John Freyer sold all of his possessions on eBay, then visited each of the more than six hundred buyers to gather material for a book called *All My Life for Sale*.

■ A man who was simply trying to get rid of a box of Beanie Babies left behind by an ex got so fed up with detailed questions from fanatic collectors that he updated his ad several times with increasingly angry suggestions that potential buyers should get a life.

- A listing for a purported "Ghost in a Jar!" with a photo ostensibly depicting just that led to spoofs including "Ghost in a Car!" that featured a picture of a PacMan character in a driver's seat.

- The photograph in an ad for a silver teapot included a faint reflection of the photographer, a male who was naked at the time. This was the first in a series of "sex sells" images that became known as "Reflectoporn." (If you have any doubt that it's caught on, try Googling that word.)

- Perhaps the most unusual item ever listed on eBay: "One soul! Get it before the devil does!"

In addition to the classes set up to appeal to groups with specific interests, there's one big gathering for everyone. It features Meg Whitman talking about a lot of the same issues she had discussed at the shareholder meeting. The difference is that this time she's doing it for thousands of people in a huge room while walking around an elaborate set featuring, among other things, a gigantic spring with the word "Leap!" on top of it.

The other difference is that while the shareholder meeting sort of petered out, there's a real showstopper of an ending here. When Whitman and the other presenters are finished, a huge gospel choir streams in from one side of the stage, white robes shimmering as they belt out an inspirational "Ain't No Mountain High Enough." Their enthusiasm is infectious, and even people heading for the exits to return phone calls or visit the bathroom can't help but sing along. "Mountain" is followed by "Down by the Riverside" and the inevitable local classic, "When the

Saints Come Marching In." During "Saints," the choir splits into two lines and parades down the aisles toward the lobby, singing and banging tambourines.

I'm still humming when I leave the convention center awhile later, carrying bags filled with a shocking number of things I don't need, don't want, and can't imagine for the life of me what I was thinking when I picked them up. Eventually it dawns on me that I know just what to do: Sell 'em on eBay!

In a nutshell . . .

EBAY

EDUCATIONAL VALUE: **B**
   Strong, clear explanations of company.
ENTERTAINMENT VALUE: **A**
   eBay Live! classes were outstanding.
FREEBIES: **A**
   T-shirt, notebook, pen (at meeting).
FOOD & DRINK: **B**
   Breakfast buffet at meeting, reception at Live!

INSIGHT: Companies have a lot of flexibility regarding where they hold their meetings. While most stick with locations relatively close to headquarters, several are peripatetic and say that moving the meeting each year gives more shareholders the opportunity to attend. There's probably some truth to that—but holding the annual gathering in an unexpected city at an early hour in a small room that's difficult to find makes it appear the company would rather not have the owners attend.

17

You Can't Always Vote if You Want

ANSELL AND BHP BILLITON

Disclosure: When I first visited Australia in 1992, I was delighted to find that a place so far away from home could feel so much like home. Yet the differences were fascinating, too. I loved jogging around the iconic Sydney Opera House, finding pumpkin soup on menus everywhere, and seeing kangaroos in the wild. I've been lucky enough to return several times since and to work with some wonderful folks there on projects for Australian investors.

My affection for the country led me to look for an Australian stock. There are quite a few available to U.S. investors, but the one that caught my eye in early 2004 was Ansell, a Melbourne manufacturer of latex gloves and condoms. The company had restructured dramatically during the previous few years, flirting with bankruptcy and getting out of the tire business that had once been its main focus. By the time I invested, Ansell was paying a good dividend and seemed to be back on the right track.

Speaking of tracks, I had become obsessed with the idea of riding a train (the Indian Pacific) across Australia—a country that's roughly the same size as the United States. So when Ansell announced its 2004 annual meeting, I made airline reservations and train reservations. While I was at it, I got in touch with the country's most notorious gadfly and he invited me to watch him in action at another company's meeting.

I had known from the start of my quest that my votes at shareholder meetings weren't likely to mean much in the grand scheme of things. Still, like a good citizen, I made it a point to cast my ballot at each opportunity.

The thing about being a citizen, of course, is you're only allowed to vote in your own country. It turns out that where you live also affects whether you can vote at shareholder meetings for companies based outside the United States.

If you own stock in foreign companies, you may be eligible to attend their shareholder meetings—typically known outside the States as AGMs (annual general meetings). Just don't expect such meetings to be like they are here at home. Customs are different, your rights are different, and you may not understand a word that's spoken.

I've just flown halfway around the world, in part to see how shareholder meetings are handled upside-down (for one thing, many of them are held in the fall—exactly the opposite of the "season" in the northern hemisphere).

I own shares in Ansell. Actually, I don't. I own American Depositary Receipts (ADRs)—certificates representing receipts for shares held by a U.S. bank. ADRs listed on the New York Stock Exchange (NYSE), the American Stock Exchange (AMEX), or NASDAQ make it possible for U.S. residents to invest in hundreds of foreign companies.[1]

---

1. More than 450, as of mid-2006. The "top ten" countries—those with the largest number of companies listed as ADRs—were the United Kingdom, China, Brazil, France, Japan, Mexico, Germany, the Netherlands, Australia, and Chile. As a group, they accounted for approximately two-thirds of all the ADRs. (There are no ADRs for Canadian companies. About 200 Canadian companies are listed directly on the NYSE, the AMEX, or NASDAQ.)

In many ways, holding ADRs isn't any different than holding shares. But there are fewer rules (sometimes none at all) requiring the company involved to invite you to the shareholder meeting—or even to tell you about it, in English or on a timely basis. I've received several notices for foreign meetings after the meetings themselves had already occurred. In fairness, most foreign companies try surprisingly hard to please their U.S. investors.

Even if you get the proxy statement in plenty of time (as I did for Ansell's meeting), and even if you return it to your broker in plenty of time to receive a letter authorizing you to vote your shares independently from how your broker votes (as I did), you might still be in for a surprise when you arrive at the registration table.

When I try to check in at Ansell's meeting, they have no idea what to do with me. They say I need authorization from Bank of New York, the custodian of the actual shares, to be able to vote in person or even to speak. I had been in touch with Ansell's investor relations people months earlier to check logistics, and no one had mentioned this potential snag. Finally someone gets the bright idea to hand me a visitor's pass. It entitles me to be a silent spectator, and nothing more.

I'm scribbling notes about this misadventure when I hear someone with a North American accent who's obviously with the company joking with a colleague. "All the rest of the criminals are back there," he says, pointing at a stage door and inviting the colleague to join him. A few minutes later I see him again and am stunned to learn he's CEO Doug Tough, a Canadian. Those are words you just don't expect to hear from a CEO these days, even though they are clearly spoken in jest.

Inside the auditorium are fewer than one hundred shareholders occupying the four hundred or so cushy black chairs. The table up front is set up to accommodate more people than I'm used to seeing there. The entire board enters the room at once—oddly, to the sounds of "Exodus"—and sits down facing the audience, Bowl America–style.

Chairman Dr. Ed Tweddell, a ruddy guy who is unmistakably a native, introduces his fellow panelists, including several nominees for board seats. I've seen enough such acknowledgments to assume that the nominees will simply stand and nod at the shareholders.

But that's not what happens!

"Could each of you please tell us a few things about yourselves?" Tweddell asks. And they do, effectively offering campaign speeches even though they're running unopposed. It's a wonderful, refreshing gesture that goes a long way toward humanizing the board and the company. One introduces himself as a "self-funded retiree," whose background includes serving as chairman of the Winemakers Association of Australia—which must be a wonderful job. Another nominee is an American in his late thirties, who gets a big laugh when he alludes to Ansell's condom business by announcing that he has "four kids, which proves I'm not a fully committed customer to one of Ansell's products." He's Michael McConnell, from Shamrock Capital—Roy Disney's money management firm. When I catch up with him after the meeting, he tells me the introductions aren't standard Aussie policy but simply an idea he had suggested for today.

The campaign speeches aren't the only eye-openers. Tweddell admits that a few years earlier, Ansell (then known as Pacific Dunlop) was struggling. He credits

Harry Boon, who recently retired as CEO, for pulling the company out of the skid. Boon oversaw "Operation Full Potential," an overhaul that involved exiting the tire business and changing the company's name in 2002 to reflect its new focus on an existing subsidiary (Ansell). "It's been quite an effort to get back to the point where we could pay dividends again," Tweddell says.

A few minutes later he explains exactly where in the annual report shareholders can find precise details about the pay packages for Boon and his replacement, Doug Tough. That's the sort of information companies in the United States generally do their best to obscure; here, it's being highlighted.

Interestingly, Boon was based in the company's offices in Red Bank, New Jersey—half a world away—and now Tough works from there. What's more, all the dollar figures I'm hearing this morning are expressed in U.S. dollars, not Australian dollars.

Much of the morning's discussion deals with two proposals to implement share buyback programs, currently all the rage among Australian companies. The notion behind the idea is that if the share price is low, the company can pay interested sellers a premium for shares that are then returned to the company's treasury, reducing the number of outstanding shares and therefore enhancing their value. Unfortunately, sometimes the shares aren't retired at all but go into a stock option plan for company executives, diluting the positive effect of the buyback for shareholders who don't sell.

Ansell's buyback offers sound reasonably generous to me, but I'm fond of the company and not interested in getting rid of my holdings—that is, until I hear Twedell talk about how the company has embraced Six Sigma. Okay, I'll sell.

Votes on the directors and the proposals involve having shareholders raise color-coded cards—except, of course, for me and my red card (which doesn't really bother me, because I had voted by mail before leaving the United States). Somehow these tallies are mingled with proxies voted before the meeting, and the results are announced right away—not as unlikely as it seems, considering that "a clear majority" is all that's needed for approvals.

Wrapping up, Tweddell tells us, "I hope you'll be able to stay and join the directors for a spot of morning tea." I do, and it's quite nice—save for the fact that the lobby where it's held reminds me of the inside of a refrigerator, all aluminum and fogged glass. When I finally do leave, I notice that the bowls of freebie gloves and condoms are nearly empty.

The next morning I'm in Sydney, reading Australian newspapers and looking for stories about the Ansell meeting. Before crossing the Pacific I had discovered an Aussie Web site called Crikey that featured colorful and opinionated on-the-spot reports from AGMs, and I got the idea that Australians pay more attention to shareholder meetings than Americans do. This morning's press coverage does nothing to convince me otherwise. There are several stories about various AGMs, and the name Jack Tilburn appears more than once. Tilburn is Australia's best-known gadfly. He's a North Sydney senior citizen who calls himself "The Corporate Terminator" and uses that term as the title of his autobiography.

I had heard about the book a few months earlier from an Australian friend, and I'd finished reading it during my flight over. Tilburn, it was obvious, was a kindred spirit to Evelyn Davis, with a great deal to say about almost anything. He writes that he began agitating at AGMs in the late 1970s and says, "I have never attended a meeting without rising to my feet. I have weathered all sorts of raw deals, excessive arrogance and contempt from dozens of chairmen." He claims credit for everything from shaming Australian companies into providing refreshments at meetings to helping eliminate three-to-five-minute time limits for shareholder remarks. He finds inspiration in a George Bernard Shaw quote: "All progress depends on the unreasonable man."

Several weeks earlier, I'd e-mailed Tilburn and he had responded that I should give him a call when I was in Sydney. A few hours before hopping aboard the Indian Pacific for a long-planned leisurely train ride across Australia, I dial Tilburn's number. He answers with a booming voice and seems to say everything twice ("Hi! Hi!" . . . "Yes, yes!" . . . "Quite right, quite right!"). I ask if he might be able to meet for a chat when I return to Sydney the following Friday. "I'm going to be at BHP Billiton's AGM that day. Why don't you join me as my guest?" he says.

I know almost nothing about BHP Billiton other than it's a mining concern and one of Australia's largest companies. But early the next morning, after spending a night bouncing through the Blue Mountains, I get a chance to learn more when my train stops for a few hours in a dusty town completely surrounded by desert. It's Broken Hill, the "BH" from the company name.

When prospectors found silver here in 1883, a group of investors bought up all the land in the area. In early 1885 they discovered one of the world's largest veins of silver, lead, and zinc—a ribbon of precious metals more than four miles long. Later that year, they incorporated as the Broken Hill Proprietary Company (BHP). By 1891 the population of the outpost known as Broken Hill had mushroomed to twenty thousand—roughly what it is today. From the start, BHP was a tough place to work. Hundreds were killed in mine accidents, and employees were even required to pay the company for the shovels they used. While there are still some mining operations in the area, BHP pulled out in 1940. A tour guide tells me locals still haven't forgiven the company: "They took our name, took our money, and did a runner," he says.

I spend the next two days rolling across the moonscape of the Australian outback, thrilled to see kangaroos hopping alongside the train and eagles soaring overhead. One of the highlights of the ride is a stretch of track that runs absolutely straight for nearly three hundred miles across the Nullarbor (Latin for "no trees") Plain.

When I had told Nancy I wanted to make this trip, I'd mentioned this straightaway, the longest of its kind anywhere. She looked at me like I was nuts and said, "And that really interests you?" I told her it did. That, plus a relatively complex itinerary involving two hemispheres, seven flights, and one three-day train ride in a total of less than two weeks might be why she had responded, "Have a good time!"

That's exactly what I'm doing. It gets even better when I arrive in Perth and pick up the car Hertz had foolishly agreed to rent me. They drive on the left in Australia, and the steering wheel is on the right—with the stick shift in the middle, under the left hand. I had coped with that once before when Nancy and I spent a few days driving around New Zealand. Sure, we turned on the windshield wipers when we meant to signal turns, but other than that the driving went pretty smoothly.

There's a lot more traffic in Perth than there was on the

south island of New Zealand. I feel like a kid who has been thrown into a lake to force him to learn to swim. Fortunately, the previous experience serves me well, save for a few unplanned windshield wipings, and three hours later I'm in the uncrowded Margaret River wine country, at the southwestern corner of the continent.

After visiting half a dozen tasting rooms—five offering wine and one, olive oil—I check in at a B&B I had reserved via the Internet a few weeks earlier. I don't usually do B&Bs, but I had figured at this point in the trip that I would need to wash my clothes, and this place advertised laundry facilities. My room, I'm dismayed to find, absolutely reeks of the most pungent potpourri imaginable. I put all my clothes, save for the ones I'm wearing, in the washer and flee in search of dinner.

An hour and a half later, with a bellyful of *nasi goreng* (Indonesian fried rice), I'm headed back to the B&B. When I stop for gas, I find out the hard way that the fit between nozzle and car isn't as snug in Australia as it is in the United States. In an instant, I'm drenched in fuel—it's soaking through my jeans, my sweatshirt, even dripping from my hair. An attendant emerges from inside the convenience store and simply stares for a minute. Then he disappears for a second and returns with a fistful of terribly inadequate paper towels that are the consistency of sandpaper. Amazingly, he doesn't laugh. I smell so strongly of gasoline that I drive away with all the windows down and still can barely breathe, but I'm patting myself on the back for having the foresight to book a place with a washer and dryer.

Until I get back to the B&B and discover that the laundry room door is shut, with a sign on the door indicating the facility is closed for the night. I pull my clothes out of the washer, figuring I can hang at least some of them up to dry in my room. Of course, when I open the door to my room, I'm knocked down by The World's Strongest Potpourri, and I realize my wet clothes will absorb the odor in seconds. So I take the basket out to my car—which smells like a refinery—and spread the wet clothes out in the trunk, hoping they'll dry overnight without collecting any of the deadly spiders or other creatures Australia has in frightening abundance. Then I head back to my room and jump in the shower fully clothed, hoping to rinse off at least some of the gasoline smell and reasoning that drying these togs in the room will work out okay because the potpourri smell will cancel out the petrol stench, more or less. When a huge thunderstorm wakes me in the middle of the night, there's still enough gas on me and in the room that if lightning strikes anywhere nearby, I figure I'm a goner.

First thing in the morning, I wrap myself in a sheet and tiptoe back to the laundry room. An hour or so later I'm good to go, although I give up on saving a favorite sweatshirt and toss it in a dumpster when I stop for lunch in tiny, charming Cowaramup.

I'm about as far from home as it's possible to be. I'm surrounded by spectacular wineries, stunning flowers, and friendly natives. The Indian Ocean is just a few miles away. The pace just couldn't be more relaxed. I over-dawdle—a mistake that leads to a white-knuckle, steering-wheel-pounding race to the airport in Perth, where I arrive fifteen minutes before my flight's scheduled departure. In my road-warrior days, I always cut it close intentionally, not wanting to waste time. But that was before 9/11 changed the rules, so I figure I'm screwed. Fortunately, the flight's running late. Unfortunately, it's after midnight by the time I get to my hotel in Sydney.

When my alarm clock sounds too few hours later, I put on my most respectable outfit that doesn't reek of gasoline and/or potpourri and catch a cab to Sydney Convention & Exhibition Centre in Darling Harbour, where I'm to meet Jack Tilburn at the BHP meeting. We hadn't established an exact spot for our rendezvous. He had simply said, "Don't worry. You'll know me."

And sure enough, I spot him almost immediately. The picture on the cover of his book is a caricature, but there's a guy who looks just like it holding court in the lobby. He's seventy or so, with white hair and one eye that doesn't seem to follow the other, wearing a green-checkered shirt with a red tie and carrying a bedraggled binder with "Corporate Terminator" written on it. As he greets a fellow shareholder by name, the response is a hearty "You're in charge, Jack!" I introduce myself and Tilburn says, "Yes, yes. It's good to meet you, good to meet you!" Suddenly I'm wondering if our get-together might last twice as long as I had figured it would.

From Tilburn's book, I know that BHP Billiton's meetings can get a bit testy: He writes that in 1995, someone with a gripe about environmental damage threw a dead fish at the chairman. When Tilburn leads us to a pair of seats near the front, we're an easy mackerel toss from a huge stage that reminds me of a Kodak film box—all yellow, orange, and black.

BHP's chairman of the board, Don Argus, got the meeting rolling with some feel-good stuff about making positive contributions to the communities where BHP operates, immediately balanced by the feel-bad admission that despite a "Zero Harm" safety program, seventeen employees have been killed on the job during the past year. President Chip Goodyear—an American who resembles Gray Davis, the former governor of California—observes that the company generated 12 percent less hazardous waste in the past year. "None of this," he adds somberly, "mitigates even one fatality."

Then Goodyear sits impassively—chewing gum, it appears—as Argus does a five-minute presentation detailing the president's pay package. What's more, it's all summarized on a slide projected on a large screen over the stage. Again I'm impressed by how forthright the Aussies are about how much the big guys get paid.

Next to me, Tilburn is muttering to himself and scribbling in his binder. One of his notes to himself reads "Keep the bastards honest!" When it's time for the Q&A, he leaps to his feet with the energy of a much younger man and launches into Argus. "You had twenty-three minutes and Chip had seventeen minutes. I wish I had that much time!" He complains bitterly that BHP's dividend is "low and miserable . . . not good enough!" and that a share buyback offer "stinks." His voice turns to a bellow, his face grows red, and his eyes begin to glow as he insists, "I speak for three hundred thousand people who aren't here. The dividend should be doubled. Did you pay a special dividend? Not bloody likely!"

I fear Tilburn's about to spontaneously combust when he finally runs out of steam, and Argus responds with a gentle "We've got your message" before moving on to a shareholder query about whether the company is sincere in efforts to repair a riverbed harmed by its operations. Goodyear offers an answer that seems smug—"We recognize our global impact. If we're inconsistent, that information is available instantly and our opportunities decrease dramatically." In other words, "the market polices us." Under his breath, Tilburn whispers, "Bloody bullshit."

There are other gadflies here, although they're all bit players compared to Tilburn. Still, they ask dozens of questions and lodge dozens of complaints, most on environmental and safety issues, over the next two hours.

I'm starving. Tilburn must be reading my mind, because he jumps into the fray again, ranting that the meeting is running long and should have been adjourned for lunch some time ago. Unfortunately, his rant takes a left-hand turn and veers into any number of other topics. "The Safety, Health, and Environment Committee should be sacked!" he bellows, as several shareholders quietly exit. "The committee is not properly functioning, with seventeen deaths! I am ashamed to be connected with BHP!"

"That's tough, Jack," says Argus, in a tone that seems simultaneously consoling and condescending.

More than a dozen items on the agenda require shareholder votes, and Tilburn rises to offer his comments on nearly every one. Each time, he's formally recognized by an attendant who introduces him—a formality that grows sillier and sillier. When votes are called for each item, Tilburn is often the only one opposing the company's recommendation.

I find myself shrinking into my seat, hoping Tilburn isn't just performing for my sake. If it's an act, it's a good one. "So greedy!" he hisses convincingly in response to one proposal. "It never ends!" he mutters about another.

But finally, it does. The next evening, I catch up with a financial industry pal who works in Sydney, and I tell him about the day with Tilburn. He just shakes his head and offers that I probably got the gist of Australian AGMs out of the experience. "I'd bet that if you wanted to see a really exotic AGM, the place to do it would be India."

Right away I imagine pageantry, elephants, and snake charmers—all of which is probably far from reality (although Tata Motors, India's largest automaker, has offered AGM attendees discounts on car loans). In any case, I think the most exotic gathering would be one where I don't speak the language and have no idea what's going on. I can be clueless almost anywhere, but it's a little more difficult to find corporate gatherings where speaking English isn't enough to get by. I own a few shares in a Hungarian phone company, largely for senti-mental reasons (my lineage is part-Hungarian), and when I look into attending the AGM I'm amazed to be told that "of course" simultaneous English translation is provided.

Of course, that's not to say translations will always be dependable. In Japan, for instance, companies offering English translations warn that the Japanese version pre-vails if there's any confusion. Actually, there's very little time for anyone to be confused: Shareholder meeting season in Japan lasts about an hour. That's because more than two-thirds of all Japanese AGMs are held in late June on exactly the same day, at exactly the same time. For decades, Japan's much-feared *sokaiya* gangsters have threatened to ask embarrassing questions at shareholder meetings unless they're paid to stay quiet. Scheduling many meetings to run concurrently dilutes the potential for any one company to be a shakedown victim, because there aren't enough gangsters to go around.

At least in Japan they actually *hold* the events. In China, Minsheng Banking faked an entire meeting in 2000 and reported that shareholders had voted in favor of a name change. The truth came out only when a director complained to the media that his signature had been forged on a document related to the meeting that was never held.

That sort of thing probably couldn't happen in Hong Kong, where AGMs are popular because they typically include a free lunch. It's not unusual for hungry shareholders to show up for the meal and skip the business end of things altogether. No doubt that's a deal some companies gladly make.

In Nepal, shareholders are even more demanding: They've been pushing companies to reimburse travel costs for attending AGMs. Unfortunately, it's just about impossible for an individual investor who lives in the United States to buy shares in a Nepalese company, so I probably won't be hiring a Sherpa anytime soon.

It would be nice if that reimbursement idea were to catch on, though, especially since the next meeting on my calendar is in one of the more expensive burgs on the planet: New York City.

In a nutshell . . .

ANSELL (AUSTRALIA)

EDUCATIONAL VALUE: **C**
  Reasonable explanations of the business.
ENTERTAINMENT VALUE: **C**
  "Campaign speeches," double entendres.
FREEBIES: **B**
  Condoms, gloves, mints.
FOOD & DRINK: **D**
  Shortbread cookies, coffee.

INSIGHT: Turning up at a shareholder meeting outside the United States is a lot like turning up at a polling place in a country you don't live in: Most of the time, they're not going to let you vote. The problem is that your "shares" are typically receipts (known as ADRs) for shares actually held by a custodian bank, which retains the voting rights. Sometimes, companies outside the United States don't even have to tell you about the annual meeting, let alone invite you—but many do.

In a nutshell . . .

BHP Billiton (Australia)*

EDUCATIONAL VALUE: C
   A fair introduction to a complicated company.

ENTERTAINMENT VALUE: C
   Would've been boring without gadflies.

FREEBIES: F
   None.

FOOD & DRINK: D
   Tea and snacks.

INSIGHT: Gadflies are pretty similar wherever you go!

*BHP Billiton is also incorporated in the United Kingdom, and each year it holds a shareholder meeting there, too. Technically, the Australian company and the U.K. company are separate entities, but they operate as a combined group and shareholders own pieces of the group, not the individual companies.

18

Talk This Way

DOW JONES

Disclosure: For the better part of three decades, one of the first things I've done each weekday is read the Wall Street Journal. *On weekends my favorite ritual is to read the issue of* Barron's *that carries the following Monday's date. Somewhere along the line I got the idea that with more people relying on their own investments to get them through retirement, the publisher of those two august newspapers— Dow Jones—couldn't go wrong. In mid-2003 I bought a few shares during what I thought was a temporary price dip. I'd like to say I bought them just to be able to attend the shareholder meeting, but that would be lying.*

There's nothing like being told you *can't* do something to make you *want* to do it. My "no talking and no voting status" in Australia reminded me that I hadn't really explored what it's like to take advantage of the opportunity to tell the people running "my" companies what I think of the job they're doing.

I have no idea what it feels like to be Evelyn Davis or Jack Tilburn. So it's time to speak up. I'm going to tell the executives of the *Wall Street Journal*'s parent company, Dow Jones, just what I think of their editorial page politics.

Dow Jones's 2005 meeting is being held somewhere in the American Indian Museum, at the southern tip of Manhattan. When I arrive, the lobby is crowded with loud junior high–age children and there's no sign of pinstripes or wingtips. A security guard directs me down a dimly lit, stone-walled spiral staircase that can only lead to a dungeon. There's no sign at the bottom, either, but eventually I find a few tables piled with various Dow Jones publications—the U.S., European, and Asian editions of the *Wall Street Journal*, plus the *Cape Cod Times*, *Far East Asian Economic Review*, and compilations of columns by two Pulitzer Prize–winning *Journal* reporters. Just past the tables is an auditorium that looks like it might ordinarily serve groups of children like the one I had encountered upstairs.

I'm about five minutes late, and whoever might've been checking credentials has abandoned his or her post, so I tiptoe in and find an empty seat.

From the left corner of the stage, the company's chairman, Peter Kann—bald, white, and wearing a dark suit—is reading in a monotone from a script letting us know how sorry he is that the stock is down 25 percent since a year ago. (Reading from a script at these meetings can be dangerous. A friend who once wrote such scripts tells a story about an oblivious executive reading the instructions "turn page" aloud.)

Kann is at a lectern adorned by a plain piece of paper that says "Dow Jones." Next to him, seated at a table, are two other executives. I have no idea who they are, because their names are written in pen on placards that couldn't possibly be read from the front row. I'm reminded of the futile, unreadable-at-speed "Garage Sale" or "Lost Pet" signs one often sees attached to telephone poles near major roads. Of course, those signs are amateur efforts. These are from people who work with type for a living!

"The fact that competitive companies have been suffering even worse results is small consolation," Kann reads. He offers a litany of hopeful catchphrases, or maybe they're catchy hope-phrases. Dow Jones is "trying to develop new revenue sources." And "leveraging the power of our brands." Also, "working on a three-year plan to generate more value for customers in existing markets." All this is in the interest, he says, of "enhancing value to core customers and shareholders."

Then he sums up major developments during the past year. The biggest news is that the *Journal* is launching a Saturday edition including more "business of life" stories and potentially opening up new opportunities for consumer advertisers. Meanwhile, the company has acquired MarketWatch, an online financial information service that Kann calls "strategically sound." And there were those two Pulitzers—one to Amy Marcus for a series on how people confront cancer and another to Joe Morganstern for movie reviews. Kann uses the mention of the coveted journalism awards as a segue to praise all of Dow Jones: "Quality and integrity are pervasive values across this company," he says. "Opinions are confined to the editorial pages, where we express them with clarity, consistency, and often courage." Hmmm. I'm pretty sure someone will have something to say about that.

There's a woman muttering in the front row. I can't quite make out what she's saying, but I get the sense the words aren't important—making a scene is. Sure enough, it's Evelyn Davis. Eventually her words drown out Kann's. It's hard to believe, but apparently she's complaining because a microphone she's been given doesn't seem to be up to her standards.

"We can hear you, Evelyn," Kann offers, gently.

"I go to about forty shareholder meetings a year, and I've never run into anything like this," Davis responds. "This is *outrageous!*"

Over the next half an hour, she weighs in with lengthy opinions on every topic Kann happens to raise—except in one case, when she spends three minutes explaining that she has no opinion. She's opposed to the nomination of a director who has been associated with Bristol Myers because of "a big mess" at the pharmaceutical company, where Davis says somebody "tried to steal my resolution on political contributions." She's against stock options. And at one point she actually says, "Now I want to bring to your attention something that has nothing to do with shareholder meetings," then launches into a diatribe that's unintelligible, at least from where I'm sitting.

Almost as unintelligible are three proposals on the agenda, all related to the Bancroft family, which owns the majority of Dow Jones's stock. One proposal would allow the family to retain voting control even if they sold off a bunch of shares. The other two would fix the number of directors at sixteen and limit the number of company managers or Bancroft family members on the board to less than half that.

Mark Boyar, whose investment firm holds nearly $6 million in Dow Jones shares, manages to be recognized long enough to make his case that Dow Jones should be sold. He announces he's going to read his letter recently published by the *Journal*. "I'll read it as quickly as I can," he reassures us. "I don't want to take as much time as Evelyn did."

Kann seizes the moment and says, "Thank you. Don't encourage her."

Boyar's letter pulls no punches. He says the company has been "an unmitigated disaster," and that "we can't understand how the Bancroft family and the board has tolerated management's ineptness for so many years." Kann responds by once again apologizing for the plummeting stock price—and by blaming his predecessors for some of the company's ills.

The final proposal on the agenda won't be very popular with Kann, because it calls for him to give up one of his two titles (CEO and chairman). Virgil Hollender, who has spent twenty-four years with the company, speaks on behalf of the Independent Association of Publishers' Employees, a union that claims to represent nearly a quarter of Dow Jones's employees. "When I started," he says in a clear, strong voice, "quality was above all. In recent years, cost cuts have forced employees to work longer and harder. I'm concerned about the effects on quality."

Journal reporter Jim Browning offers some similar thoughts. "I spoke here a year ago about the contract dispute [which saw, among other things, reporters refusing to put their bylines on stories], and I wish I could tell you things have gotten better. Employees were shocked at how much the company has taken away. They've seen insurance and health benefits lost. Morale in the newsroom has continued to deteriorate, and many reporters are preparing for a fight over working conditions when the Saturday edition begins. I'm very much afraid the company is on a collision course with its most valuable assets."

Davis can't resist, of course. "I've seen this proposal at several companies. Many companies have the same person as the chairman and the president. We may have a difference of opinion, but it's not that bad. At some companies where we've had this resolution, I submitted it myself."

All I can make of that is that if she had submitted it here, she would be in favor. I think.

Before I've made any progress sorting it out, she's on the attack again, accusing the company—"Dow Chose," she pronounces it—of besmirching her reputation by running stories written by a female reporter whose last name happens to be Davis. "No relation!" she howls. *"Outrageous!"*

Kann tries to placate her by observing that he checked stories that ran on the Dow Jones newswire during the past twelve months and, "There were fourteen mentions of you. I thought you'd be pleased with us this year!" Davis keeps right on talking: "Why do you write about institutional investors? Why not write about winners like me, not losers like them? All their proposals fail. Institutions are losers, not newsworthy."

It's not looking good for me to get a word in edgewise. But finally I get Kann's attention, and when he recognizes me I decide that if Davis starts talking again I'll tell her to put a sock in it.

"I think *Barron's* is the best publication there is," I begin, nervously. "And I think that the news and feature writing in the *Journal* are generally top-notch. That's why I find it so appalling that the contents of the editorial page in the *Journal* invariably appear to have been dictated by Dick Cheney directly from his undisclosed location."

I'm surprised when the room erupts with laughter and amazed to feel that the crowd—if not the folks up front—is supportive. I finish with "Please consider that not all *Journal* readers become right-wing Republicans as they age."

This gets applause! But not from aging right-wing Republican Kann, who admits, "Well, *I* did," before asking if anyone will move to adjourn the meeting. Davis grabs the opportunity to get the last word and loudly shouts, "I so move!"

Afterward, someone wearing a badge around his neck—perhaps a *Journal* reporter?—tells me he loved my comment and disappears into the crowd.

I leave feeling good about having spoken my mind, and about having the opportunity to do so at the shareholder meeting. Just in time, too, because I'm about to fly to London and discover that no matter which ocean you cross, your shareholder credentials don't mean much on the other side.

In a nutshell . . .

DOW JONES

EDUCATIONAL VALUE: C
> Average overview, confusing proposals.

ENTERTAINMENT VALUE: C
> Enhanced by outspoken shareholders.

FREEBIES: C
> *Wall Street Journal*, *Barron's*, other papers.

FOOD & DRINK: C
> Pastries, coffee, OJ, sodas.

INSIGHT: If you own all of a small business and you don't like the way your employees are doing things, it's up to you to tell them. The principle is the same if you own a small portion of a big business.

19

Breaking Up Isn't Hard to Do

INTERCONTINENTAL HOTELS GROUP

Disclosure: My best friend's son observes that the name of a hotel chain is often the polar opposite of what it should be. If a place is called the Sleeptight Hotel, for instance, bedbugs are likely. Yet I've always associated Holiday Inns with actual holidays, because when I was a kid we stayed at them when we would travel to Florida for Easter, Thanksgiving, or Christmas. After 9/11 it seemed likely that more vacations would involve highway travel. I decided that would be good for Holiday Inns and bought shares in the parent company, a British concern now called Intercontinental Hotels Group but then known as Six Continents. (Just previously, it had been Bass, a holding company named for the brewery that was once its core property.)

I know the math won't support this, but I've always had this feeling that I'll age more gradually if I celebrate the "0" birthdays in Europe. A few months before the most recent of those, I discovered that my one British holding, Intercontinental Hotels, couldn't have scheduled its 2005 AGM more conveniently.

In the name of research (and not going broke at a time when the dollar's struggling versus the pound), Nancy and I are staying at Holiday Inns during our weeklong visit to the United Kingdom. I've stayed at quite a few in the United States lately and have been impressed. But budget London hotels have a way of disappointing, and even the Holiday Inn in tony Mayfair suffers from concave mattresses and odd touches like having the hairdryer attached to the inside of a desk drawer.

Unfortunately, I'm in no position to say a word about such concerns at the AGM, held at a futuristic conference center directly opposite Westminster Abbey. Once again, the fact that my shares are actually ADRs held by Bank of New York means that I can look but I'd better not speak (or vote). I'm given a big red "guest" card at the registration desk.

While waiting for the meeting to get under way, I chat with George Harrington, a retired British gentleman who says he attends a dozen or so AGMs each year because he likes to see what the chairman of each company is like. "If he knows everything or can point to someone at the front table who does, I'm impressed. If he's clueless, I'm worried." He tells me he was charmed when the chairman of Whitbread—a U.K.-based hotel and restaurant company—shook the hand of everyone attending that company's meeting. I tell him how Chad Holliday did the same thing at DuPont's.

Harrington's a little annoyed with Intercontinental Hotels, because the hotel directories on the information table list only North American locations. Even at that, they're as thick as phone books.

So are the meeting materials. That's because today's get-together is a "three-fer"—the normal business event plus two functions necessary to complete a complex restructuring of the company. In effect, the first meeting will deal with the existing company, the second will end the life of the existing company, and the third will create a new company that goes by the original name—all without a break.

Chairman David Webster is one of ten IHG executives on the stage, all wearing charcoal gray suits in sharp contrast to the yellow and blue backdrop. He stands and looks out over the sea of a thousand or so folding chairs—only half of which are occupied by shareholders. Webster, who looks a bit like Warren Buffett himself, with bushy eyebrows and glasses with thick frames, knows the reorganization—the second in just three years—is confusing to investors. So he talks about it right away: "I can only apologize to you for the unavoidable complexity and say that I wish we could have made things simpler for you, and ourselves."

He explains that when IHG was spun off from Six Continents, the board began reviewing the company's hotels all over the world. They concluded the company's strength was managing properties, not building and owning them. "So we decided that instead of investing large amounts in bricks and mortar, we'll do what we're best at—operating hotels," Webster says. That led to selling hundreds of properties, which meant the company needed less cash for renovations. Some of the money was returned to shareholders in the form of a special dividend, and some was used to fund a buyback program.

In the interest of getting other inevitable questions out of the way, Webster notes that a year earlier he had been asked why there wasn't a hotel discount for shareholders attending the AGM. He explains that the company could only offer discounts at hotels it owns, and there aren't many of those anymore. There's also the thorny issue of fairness: giving shareholders attending the meeting a break on rates would cost all shareholders, so those not attending might feel cheated.

Finally, he talks about how the company has recently changed CEOs. He praises the deposed Richard North as "the right man at the time," but says, "We needed new skills." When he says the board wanted someone with "branding experience," I shudder, sharing some of Roy Disney's feelings about branding. They found Andy Cosslett, who had been president of Cadbury Schweppes. "I would now very much like to hand you over to Andy Cosslett," Webster says.

Cosslett, fiftyish with thinning hair, does a brief presentation on his "early impressions" since joining the company four months earlier. Somehow I'm less than surprised that he cites features like "committed organization, management depth, well-respected brand portfolio, and sound owner relationships." I'm not the only one. None of the directors seem to be paying the least bit of attention, and when I look around I see that at least half a dozen of my fellow shareholders have nodded off.

When Cosslett's finished, shareholders seek Webster's attention by holding up the yellow voting cards everyone (except me) was given when they arrived. The chairman takes a few questions without incident, then says, "Let me go to the gentleman I cut off rather rudely last year. I assure you that won't happen again."

He's talking about a portly Indian man in the front row, who responds with "I have about five questions to ask." Almost as one, the audience shouts, "No! *One* question!" The guy carries on as if he hasn't heard the objections and works through his list. Webster eventually says, "Your *last* question, sir?"

Four questions later the gadfly attacks Webster's compensation—nearly seven hundred thousand dollars in U.S. terms. Again there's an eruption from the crowd. Somehow it's a very British outburst, all murmuring and cries of "Hear! Hear!" An ancient, shaky guy in a creatively mismatched suit totters to his feet a few rows in front of me and shouts, "Is he a *plant?*" several times. A director explains that Webster's job is increasingly onerous (and judging by what the chairman is going through right now, it's hard to disagree), so the company's compensation committee believes he's properly rewarded. Webster turns to his nemesis with a huge grin and says, "Thank you. I'll look forward to seeing you again *next* year!"

A large, blustery bald man stands, holding the company's annual report, and announces, "I'm a scientist. One of the mysteries of the world is accounting. On page fifteen, what is *negative* goodwill?" Webster gets a big laugh by responding, "The opposite of *positive* goodwill!" before adding, "I have every sympathy. These are technical documents, and for us to put into plain English the same material would take twice the space, so we accept standard accounting conventions."

He cheerfully works his way through a few more questions and then calls for votes on the directors up for election. The balloting reminds me of what I had seen in Australia. With each issue, Webster asks shareholders in favor to raise their yellow cards and then asks those against to do the same. Although there are no more than a few hundred people in the room, vote totals in the millions appear on a screen behind Webster almost simultaneously. (Later I talk with the company secretariat, Richard Winter, and he explains that voting by holding a card in the air "is a bit of theater associated with AGMs."

The vast majority of votes are cast in advance by mail or via the Internet, but those results aren't presented until meeting attendees have had the opportunity to "interface directly with the board," as Winter puts it. Interestingly, each card counts as one vote, regardless of how many shares the holder owns. In the unlikely event that the result of the show of hands differs from the result of votes cast before the meeting, the latter prevails.)

When the balloting is complete, Webster says that concludes the business of the annual meeting and reaches for a yellow binder. "Now we'll move on to the first of our extra shareholder meetings," he says. It's called a Court Meeting because the High Court of Justice in England and Wales requires it in this situation.

Webster explains the plan (here it's called a "scheme," which would raise dubious eyebrows in the United States) to have the existing company, Intercontinental Hotels Group, purchased for shares and approximately £1 billion ($1.8 billion) cash by "New Intercontinental Hotels Group." Then "New IHG" would revert to the original name immediately. Why is all of this necessary? "Unfortunately, the mechanics are much more complicated to return capital than they were for the special dividend last year, thus we're creating New IHG. In essence, New IHG will acquire old IHG for a combination of shares and cash. The cash represents the amount being returned to the shareholders. The market value of new IHG shares should be approximately the same as for existing shares. This is purely a structural change," he tells us. But it's certainly not an easy one to understand. Referring to the dense legal filing, he apologizes again: "I do appreciate that this is not the easiest document to get through. I do appreciate that it is daunting."

When he calls for a vote, cards are flashed and the proposal passes.

Webster segues to the last of this morning's three official events, the Extraordinary General Meeting—where the idea, I think, is that shareholders decide whether the proposal they just approved should be implemented. Before the vote, a tiny old woman behind me raises her hand. She protests that if you've owned the stock through all the recent reorganizations, calculating capital gains tax on sales "is a very formidable bit of arithmetic!" Webster responds, "We'll put a calculator on our Web site," and the woman sputters, "We haven't got computers!"

There's a proper tea waiting after we adjourn, with pastries and cheese-and-pickle sandwiches cut in quarters. Some shareholders I had seen napping inside are wide-awake now and happily loading their plates. "They're all bachelors," explains the feisty woman who is computer-free. Her name's Ann Comber. She's in her eighties and lives in North London on income from stocks her late husband had purchased long ago. Ann's here with her pal Maura Knight, an elderly widow from southwest London. The two met at an AGM years ago and now they get together at a dozen meetings each spring, Ann says.

The gatherings are a social outlet for them and provide unusual conversation fodder. Comber tells me, "Some woman got up at the meeting for Marks & Spencer [a British department store chain] and said she couldn't get bras to fit her. Well, *that* got in the papers!"

Knight says that food also draws the women to AGMs: "Marks & Spencer gives a box with lunch in it. So does BP [British Petroleum]." Their favorite meeting is Unilever's, because they're big fans of subsidiary Ben & Jerry's frozen concoctions. "We always go and have a whole lot of free ice cream," she says, grinning. (When Ben & Jerry's was still an independent company, founder Ben Cohen liked to sing his way through the formal part of the shareholder meeting. When he made a motion to adjourn, a group of employees would respond in kind with a melodic adaptation of an old Smokey Robinson song: "I second that motion!")

The ladies like goodie bags and freebies, too. "One day last week we had ICI [chemicals] in the morning and Glaxo [pharmaceuticals] in the afternoon," Comber says. "Glaxo is mean. They only gave you a cup of tea. ICI had bottles full of stuff to paint on fences. I had a shed that needed doing, so I took a bunch of them."

I'm tickled by the notion of this energetic octogenarian loading up on cans of paint. There's something wonderful about freebies from shareholder meetings, no doubt about it. My own hauls have included, among other things, toothpaste, boxes of pasta, picture frames, coupons for several years' worth of frozen nondairy treats, and so many pens and notepads that I'll probably never buy either again. (Alas, I never owned shares in Alderwoods Group, a funeral home chain recently taken over by Service Corporation International, which dominates the death care industry. Apparently, Alderwoods raised an eyebrow or two by giving away coffin-shaped chocolate bars.)

Are goodie bags and freebies at shareholder meetings unfair to those who don't attend? I doubt it very much. In most cases the dollar value is minimal. And if trinkets somehow help to lure more people to the annual face-to-face with the company's management, it's possible that all shareholders are better served.

In a nutshell . . .

INTERCONTINENTAL HOTELS GROUP

EDUCATIONAL VALUE: **C**
  Murky explanations of constant reorganizations.
ENTERTAINMENT VALUE: **B**
  Amusing "Hear! Hear!" atmosphere.
FREEBIES: **F**
  None (except catalog of Holiday Inns in the United
  States!)
FOOD & DRINK: **B**
  Post-meeting brunch pastries, sandwiches, etc.

INSIGHT: Special shareholder meetings (often called "extraordinary" meetings outside the United States) are typically held when a merger or major restructuring is in the works.

20

You Say You Want a Resolution

CITIGROUP

Disclosure: *For many years, I've carried a Citi credit card that includes a nifty identity-theft prevention device: my picture. Periodically Citi sends me a new card, but it always features the same old photo, so I look great for my age. Alas, Citi squandered a lot of goodwill after a few years when it started barraging me with offers to "protect" my credit. Invariably they arrived in envelopes prominently marked "Check Enclosed," and cashing the check would start my subscription to the service. Several times I asked Citi to take me off their list, but the junk mail kept coming. Frustrated, I finally wrote this letter to the then-president and CEO of Citibank, a division of parent company, Citicorp:*

> *Today I received a solicitation for your Citibank Credit Protector service in an envelope boasting "Check Enclosed." This is a blatantly irresponsible, public invitation for any potential identity thief, and I have previously asked Citibank to stop sending me such mailings. You've ignored my requests. I'm going to send you this response in an envelope conspicuously marked "V.D. Test Results Inside." Because your mailing didn't offer a complete address for you, I'll have to send it to whatever mailroom I can find for Citibank—so quite a few people may see it before it reaches you. Perhaps this will help you understand how I feel about your tactics.*

I mailed the letter, marked (in red) as promised, and whadya know? The unwanted invitations ceased immediately. But I was still wary when I bought some Citigroup stock a few years later, attracted by the dividend and by the prospect of a shareholder meeting that's often a lightning rod for shareholder proposals.

How do you get to Carnegie Hall? Well, you could heed that groan-worthy advice to "practice, practice, practice." Or you could buy a few shares in Citigroup, which holds its shareholder meeting at the famous venue.

That's what I did, and it's why I'm shivering on a Manhattan sidewalk one morning in April 2006. The line in front of me is moving at a glacial speed, because each of the one thousand or so Citigroup shareholders here for chairman Sandy Weill's last hurrah has to clear a security checkpoint. As we wait, a guy walking by on his way to work raises an eyebrow at the crowd and asks me what's going on. "Citigroup," I tell him. "Business meeting, sounds boring," he responds. "Actually, it's the shareholder meeting. Could be exciting," I say. He brightens and comes back with "That's more like it!"

Well, here's hoping. I'd hate to see a bad performance at Carnegie Hall.

What's a shareholder meeting doing in a place like this, anyway? As it happens, Weill is the answer to that question. He chairs the Carnegie Hall board of directors and has been a major benefactor. The building includes a Citigroup Café and a Joan and Sanford I. Weill Recital Hall.

Today's function is in the Isaac Stern Auditorium, the largest of Carnegie Hall's three stages. The auditorium rivals the DuPont Theatre. There are one thousand seats on the main floor, all red and plush. Above, four tiers of balconies—the top one requiring a climb of 105 steps—accommodate another eighteen hundred. The ceiling features concentric circles of 128 lights more than eighty feet overhead, and I wonder how they replace the bulbs when they burn out. (There's a catwalk hidden in the ceiling, I learn later.) The stage looks like one you'd see at an elementary school in a well-off place: I keep expecting a bunch of earnest, singing six-year-olds dressed like pieces of fruit to emerge from the double doors at each side.

Atop the small table onstage there are two name cards, easily readable from the middle of the room, where I've found a seat. One card says "Sanford Weill"—the guy who everyone calls Sandy. The other says "Charles Prince" and it's for the Weill protégé who is taking over as Citigroup's chairman after this meeting. The only other signage is a small, barely visible corporate logo on a piece of white paper attached to the front of a lectern.

It occurs to me that Citigroup's meeting marks the first I've been to for a company with a one-letter stock symbol (an abbreviation used to make trading easier)—C, in this case. In all, there are fifteen companies with one-letter symbols, including Ford (F), Kellogg (K), AT&T (T) and U.S. Steel (X). A one-letter symbol is sort of the equivalent of a single-digit address. But the symbols G, H, I, J, M, P, U, W, and Z are all up for grabs. (For years, I've threatened to put together a company called Grossmismanagement Enterprises. I'm not at all sure what the company might do, but if it ever goes public I've got my eye on that G symbol.)

When two elderly women take the seats next to me, I make small talk with one, asking if she's been to other shareholder meetings here. "Oh, yes," she says. "Citi's had its meeting here for years." (Not since the beginning, though. Citibank, the ancestor of Citigroup, got started in 1812. Carnegie Hall was built in 1890.)

"It's quite a place," I offer, understating the obvious. "The acoustics are marvelous," she responds. Of course, they're probably wasted on an event like this, we agree, as Chuck Prince slowly wanders onstage looking a little lost. Eventually he reaches the microphone and says, "To conduct his final shareholder meeting as chairman of the board of Citigroup, Sandy Weill!" That's the cue for Weill's fans—and there are many in the room—to give the departing executive a standing ovation.

I'm wondering if this gathering will be a glowing, all's-right-with-the-world sendoff like I had seen in October 2004 at Paychex's shareholder meeting in Rochester, New York. That company's CEO/chairman/president, Tom Golisano, had stepped down five weeks after getting remarried at the age of sixty-three, expressing an understandable desire to spend more time in a warmer climate. When he came onstage to thunderous applause, Golisano responded with a reference to a recent event under the same roof: "The Bette Midler concert was *last* night!" Paychex employees who spoke during the meeting all used the occasion to lionize the outgoing executive, and most of the shareholder questions were lobs.

Weill beams as he takes the stage, and thirty seconds pass before he speaks. He's not a big man, but his voice fills the hall as he introduces Prince and the company's directors, which include Robert Rubin (secretary of the treasury under Bill Clinton) and Dick Parsons (chairman and CEO of Time Warner), among others. When each gets prolonged applause, it occurs to me this could be a long meeting.

Among other items on the agenda, there are seven shareholder proposals listed. The only other meeting I've attended where there were so many was Wal-Mart's. Like Wal-Mart, Citigroup is a target that draws a lot of fire.

Shareholders—or at least the activist groups and foundations typically behind proposals—seem antsier in 2006, although according to Institutional Shareholder Services the number of proposals filed has been pretty steady since 2003 (between 1,000 and 1,100 filed annually, with slightly more than half actually going to a vote). More than 120 of this year's proposals would require that directors receive an actual majority of votes cast to be elected. It's become a popular idea (despite the fact that a few years ago the Business Roundtable—a group of CEOs from America's largest companies—insisted that making votes for directors meaningful would confuse shareholders, increase costs, and result in less-qualified boards). Many companies have simply agreed to make the change without a fight, while others—including ExxonMobil and GM—have taken shareholder votes to heart. Other especially popular themes for shareholder proposals this year deal with political contributions, labor standards, and global warming. The number of proposals at some 2006 meetings reaches into double digits: there are fifteen at Dow Chemical's gathering.

Weill knows that this morning's agenda is packed, so it's hard to fault him for trying to rush. But he's in trouble from the start. As soon as he asks if anyone has any comments on the first agenda item—reelecting the company's sixteen directors to one-year terms—there are lines at the microphones.

A mustached shareholder who clearly has a history with

Weill complains vigorously that many Citigroup directors sit on too many other corporate boards to be truly attentive and effective. He insists the limit should be two. Then he turns to face the crowd and asks, "How many people here don't work for Citigroup?" Most of the seven or eight hundred people in the room raise their hands. I'm not sure what that proves, but Weill's nemesis turns back to the chairman and says triumphantly, "What do you think about *that?*"

"About whether all these people should work for Citigroup?" Weill asks, seeming as mystified as I am.

Mr. Mustache doesn't like that response and spits back, "I'd love to work for Citicorp and get some of your money!"

Weill launches into a superlative-filled defense of the company's board, essentially saying all of the directors are among the finest people ever born. Then he observes that anyone who has been invested in Citigroup for a while has made a lot of money. "I encourage you to enjoy the journey," he concludes.

Again, that sets off Mr. Mustache. "The journey has not been good over recent years," he says. Then he reads off a long list of dates spanning quite a few years and says the stock price has been more or less the same on each one of them.

Weill looks thoughtful and responds: "You left out the most important date: Three thirteen oh-seven."

"What's coming then?" asks the unhappy shareholder.

"Wait and see," teases Weill. Okay, maybe . . . just *maybe* . . . Weill knows of something that will give the stock price a big boost nearly a year in the future. Somehow, though, I doubt it. I'm guessing it's nothing more than a clever bit of bullshit intended to derail his interrogator. In any case, Weill is able to turn away and recognize a young woman standing at a microphone on the other side of the auditorium.

She's one of a dozen or so people here today speaking on behalf of various union pension funds with investments in Citicorp. None are happy, most are strident, and nearly all seem poorly rehearsed, surprised by their own scripts.

The accusations fly and Weill deals with all of them in pretty much the same way—using no end of superlatives to characterize Citigroup's people and procedures as second to none.

When there's a complaint about a Citi employee in Argentina helping someone move money out of that country without paying taxes, Weill says, "Our bank has the best anti–money laundering procedures in the business."

When a near-hysterical spokeswoman who seems incapable of using contractions raises Citi's loans to Enron via offshore entities and suggests director Rubin should have stopped such things, Weill says, "Bob Rubin was maybe the greatest secretary of the treasury this county has ever had. Citigroup is fortunate to have him on the board . . . yadda, yadda, yadda. . . ." He begs off talking about Enron, citing ongoing litigation, and gets a sympathetic laugh from some of the crowd when he adds, "You're making me glad I'm retiring!"

Still another earnest, young female union rep cycles back to the complaint that serving on too many other boards distracts Citigroup's directors. Some, she says, are on thirteen or fourteen boards, and one is on nineteen. Weill objects that she's including nonprofit boards (as if they require no time or attention!) and says Citigroup has no policy on other commitments. "We benefit from the knowledge our directors get from serving on other boards," he insists.

And right then, in Carnegie Hall with its perfect acoustics, my cell phone rings—cranking out a cheesy rendition of "When the Saints Come Marchin' In." Fortunately, it's in my briefcase as it erupts, and that muffles most of the sound as I flee the room. My only consolation is that I've already heard several other phones ringing, proving I'm not a solo idiot and that maybe those customary premeeting warnings to turn 'em off aren't a waste of time after all. (There wasn't one here.)

When I return a few minutes later, Weill is defending another board member: "Mike Armstrong [former chairman and CEO at AT&T] does a phenomenal job. Any director would say there's no better director to work with."

There have been so many director-related questions and comments it's hard to blame the next shareholder to the microphone when he attempts to change the subject. First, he vents a little about how the union spokespeople seem to be hogging the spotlight: "Unfortunately, I don't represent one hundred million shares of anybody's." Then he tells us how he recently returned from an overseas trip where he had used his Citibank card quite often, only to find he'd paid a 3 percent charge for currency conversions. He thinks the charge is unconscionable.

Of course, his complaint doesn't have anything to do with nominations for the board, which are currently on the table for discussion. So Weill tries to shoo the man away by referring him to "the customer service representatives in the back of the room," but the shareholder doesn't back down. "This is a matter that affects *every* customer!" he says angrily, adding that the charges were disclosed "on those little pieces of paper mailed with statements, where the type is so tiny we can't read it." Weill sighs and says, "We'll take a look at it."

Then Mr. Mustache returns, complaining that Weill profited from a Citigroup stock buyback. Weill retaliates,

"You and every other shareholder have the right to take advantage of the buyback. For somebody like myself, who has a disproportionate amount in Citigroup stock—I've never bought any other stock—I should be allowed to diversify. That doesn't mean I don't have confidence in the future of the company." On a roll, he continues, "No company has ever delivered as much for the shareholders as this company has."

Mr. Mustache is exasperated: "If everything's so good, why is the stock price static?" he says, more as a statement than a question. "See ya!" he adds.

"I can't wait," Weill says.

Nobody has any comments about the proposal to reappoint the company's outside auditors, KMPG, which has reviewed the books of Citigroup and its predecessors since 1969. I'm a little surprised, because in the wake of the Enron accounting scandals many companies have made it a point not to get too cozy with outside auditors—often changing auditors every few years. But part of the collateral damage from Enron was the demise of Arthur Andersen, which had served as Enron's auditor. The loss of Andersen, which had been one of the "Big Five" accounting firms, means there are fewer options for a company like Citicorp.

Similarly, no one says a peep about three company-sponsored proposals to make minor reductions in the number of votes needed to approve ideas like issuing new shares or amending the company's bylaws.

The first shareholder-sponsored proposal is from Evelyn Davis, "who is not able to be with us today," Weill says. There's a sigh of relief from those who know Davis's absence means we're more likely to be out of here in time for lunch.

Davis's proposal—to ban Citigroup from awarding stock options—doesn't seem unreasonable to me. Neither do the proposals that follow—to require the company to disclose political contributions and charitable gifts, to tie executive compensation to performance, to have the company reimburse shareholders for expenses they incur contesting a board seat, to require that the chairman not hold any other management position at Citicorp, and to require management to give back bonuses based on earnings if those earnings are "restated" (adjusted, almost certainly downward) at a later date.

As usual, most of the people who rise to speak on behalf of the proposals aren't skilled persuaders (of course, with the vast majority of shares voted ahead of the meeting, it's probably a little late for that to matter). They fumble, they drone, they shriek. Only one—the advocate for relating pay to results—abandons his script and speaks from the heart; it's a refreshing break. (Interestingly, it's the one shareholder proposal that comes very close to passing. When the votes are announced at the end of the meeting, percentages of opposing votes are cited for the other proposals, but not this one. It's said to have failed for "no clear majority." The words are so carefully chosen that it's no surprise when a shareholder presses for details and a Citigroup spokesman says the vote ran 48 percent for and 49 percent against.)

Weill advises anyone who wants to cast a ballot here at the meeting to do it now. After a pause for attendants to collect paper ballots from the few who didn't mail their votes in earlier, he adds, "I'm now going to say six words that'll change my life: I now declare the polls closed."

Chuck Prince takes over, and just as he's launching into a "State of the Citi" report, two cell phones ring almost in unison. I feel incrementally less embarrassed.

When Prince starts to talk about the company's results over the past year, a slide appears on a center panel behind the stage. The panel's relatively big and so is the projected image. Unfortunately, the type on the slide is not and the audience squints as one. Prince looks surprised but recovers quickly. "We have a teeny, tiny slide," he says. "The numbers are actually much bigger than they are up there!" That gets a small laugh, but the unintentional eye test is a frustrating faux pas.

I'm guessing the slide was put together by a graphic designer who is still many years away from bifocals and figures everyone's vision is twenty-twenty. Making the situation worse, the designer opted for wide margins to provide some "white space"—forgetting, perhaps, that the entire back wall of the stage was already white, so making the type larger and taking it right to the edge of the slide would have worked just fine.

Prince gets through the numbers and starts talking about Citigroup employees who responded to needs for help after Hurricane Katrina devastated the Gulf Coast and a tsunami killed tens of thousands in Asia. He introduces a short video that includes an image of someone holding a sign that says, "Thank you CITIGROUP volunteers!" It's hard not to be suspicious of a sign that so clearly highlights the company's name. Still, whoever put it together did a better job than whoever created today's slides.

The rest of the meeting is all about looking backward—reviewing Sandy Weill's career in the financial business. For over half a century, Weill has been instrumental in a dizzying number of mergers of brokerages, insurance companies, consumer finance companies, and banks. The biggest was the 1998 marriage of Travelers Group and Citicorp—a risky endeavor that involved a successful bet on Congress lifting a sixty-four-year-old prohibition on banks, brokerages, and insurance companies getting into one another's businesses. Today, Citigroup's logo incorporates the old red umbrella symbol that had represented Travelers. (Indeed, the only freebie at today's meeting is a tiny red umbrella lapel pin.)

Most of the shareholders who line up at the microphones for what would ordinarily be a typical Q&A have come to praise Weill. One particularly bubbly woman fawns that the outgoing chairman is "the best corporate leader ever" and "absolutely awesome" before concluding, "We'll always be proud of you." Except she's not finished yet. "And now I'd like to read a little poem I wrote!" she chirps like a teenage girl with a hopeless crush. A few seats away from me, someone mutters, "Oh, God," and small groups of people begin to head for the exits.

"Dear Sandy Weill," she begins. "We love your style. You're the best in the biz as far as I can tell. You've made us all richer and we've all done quite well." There are several verses, all dripping with words like "glow" and "brilliance." At long last, she says, "The End." But she's still not finished: "And I'm gonna put a P.S. on that poem!" precedes a few more flirtatious comments.

Weill's delighted until he sees who's next at the microphone. "I could never do anything like that," Mr. Mustache says. "You could *try*!" Weill quickly responds, and everyone laughs.

Mustache commends the investor relations department at Citigroup for prompt responses when he's had questions, and he praises his local Citibank branch. Oddly, he finishes by advising Prince to "Watch out for China. Time means *nothing* to them."

An out-of-breath older man who has just come through

the back doors rushes to the microphone. He introduces himself as "a good friend of the Bushes" and seems to be announcing a personal campaign to get the government to investigate Citigroup's credit card rates. He says rising rates cause high rates of defaults and hurt the economy. Even the shareholders who've spent the morning criticizing Citigroup seem to react as though this guy's peeing in the community pool. Prince says there's currently an "oversupply" in the credit card industry and that it's causing rates to go down, not up.

Quickly he segues to a closing tribute to Weill. The Citigroup board, he announces, has voted to recognize Weill by naming him chairman emeritus and donating $5 million to benefit a Tanzanian medical school that is a favorite Weill charity. Then the lights go down and Dan Rather is onscreen, asking, "Who do you know that's touched more people than Sandy Weill?" The video tribute includes appearances by Yo-Yo Ma (who says, "If Sandy were a piece of music, he might sound like this," and then plays an obviously complex bit), New York City mayor Michael Bloomberg, and Citigroup director emeritus Gerald Ford (who comments, "Sandy and I both married above ourselves"), plus Weill's wife, Joan, and their two children, and there are lots of images of Weill moving and shaking with the likes of Bill Clinton and Paul McCartney. The focus is on Weill's efforts for charity.

When the lights come back up, Weill gets a standing O. He starts to offer some farewell remarks but doesn't get far before he chokes up and sobs. "I can't do it!" he says and pauses for a few seconds to regain his composure. He doesn't quite succeed, and there are a few more awkward moments. At one point he talks about a business "where we started with four people and a lady." A minute or two later he tells a group of children sitting up front, "You've learned a little bit this morning by seeing 'democracy' in action," using his fingers to form quote marks gently mocking the notion of shareholder voting. And he finishes with an odd slap at Prince: "Most of all I feel incredibly good about this little heavy-set lawyer from Baltimore who ate more French-fried potatoes and hamburgers than anybody else I've ever seen."

Prince gracefully responds, "Except for the cheap shot about the French fries, I thought that was very nice." Then we're adjourned, but he invites us all to stay for a few minutes to have our collective picture taken with Sandy and Joan Weill. The retiring chairman and his wife stand with their backs to us as a photographer onstage tries to make the most of the scene.

Heading out, I follow the crowd, figuring most people are probably as hungry as I am and eager to get some lunch. There was no mention of Citigroup feeding us— indeed, today's meeting is the only one I can ever remember attending where there wasn't even complimentary coffee—so I'm guessing we're headed for an exit. Halfway down a narrowing hallway lined with music charts and letters signed by composers like Rachmaninoff and Dvorak, I realize that I'm in a line of shareholders who want to shake Weill's hand and say good-bye.

Some, no doubt, are Weill's friends. Others are Average Joes and Janes who on any other day of the year would have had a mighty tough time trying to chat with the top man at one of the world's largest companies. I'm reminded once again that shareholder meetings can provide individual investors with unique access to the executives who work for them.

The odds are pretty good that Poetry Lady and Mr.

Mustache are somewhere ahead of me, so I decide it might be quite a wait. As I turn to go, I catch a final glimpse of Weill, who's laughing and having a wonderful time. It's been a challenging day for the outgoing chairman and CEO of Citigroup, but I suspect he'll miss all of this very much.

In a nutshell . . .

CITIGROUP

EDUCATIONAL VALUE: **C**
   Much ado about Weill, not much about Citigroup.
ENTERTAINMENT VALUE: **A**
   Hour-long film, various sideshows.
FREEBIES: **F**
   Red umbrella lapel pin.
FOOD & DRINK: **F**
   None.

INSIGHT: When a longtime chairman or CEO retires, the shareholder meeting is a likely occasion for a public tribute.

21

Sweet Somethin's
TOOTSIE ROLL

Disclosure: Nothing ranked higher than Tootsie Rolls in the Halloween hauls of my youth. Decades later I noticed that the company itself ranked very high in terms of long-term "total return"—share price appreciation plus dividends. One reason: Tootsie Roll has paid dividends since the 1940s and a 3 percent "share dividend" (100 shares becomes 103) every year since 1965. When the stock price seemed appetizing in mid-2005, I took a bite.

I t's a school day, but ten-year-old Andy Ross and eleven-year-old Will Christ are skipping classes with parental permission. They live in suburban Washington, D.C., but their parents have driven them one hundred miles south to Richmond, Virginia, so that the youngsters can get a taste of the business world by visiting Tootsie Roll's 2006 shareholder meeting. Both boys own stock in the company and are, by all accounts, enthusiastic consumers of its products.

They're among a dozen or so investors and a like number of Tootsie Roll employees gathered in the cramped twelfth-floor conference room of an old bank building. All of us, regardless of age, are hungrily eyeing the huge assortment of the company's candies strewn across a long shelf under the windows. Any chance, we're all thinking, that when the meeting is over, they'll let us take some of those "samples" home?

Will, who is directly in front of me, is studying the display intently, and he explains that he's looking for Cry Baby Extra Sour gumballs—which are, he thinks, the best candy ever made. He's sitting with his mom, Susan, and a friend of hers, investment adviser Ingrid Hendershot. Chatting with the two women before the meeting begins, I learn that they were both in Omaha last spring for Berkshire Hathaway's shareholder meeting. It was the tenth time around for Hendershot. "*This* meeting is very different!" she says.

As we're talking, the two top executives of Tootsie Roll get comfortable behind the table at the front. Melvin Gordon, a spry 86, is the company's chairman and CEO. He is quite possibly the oldest active CEO of a public company (although he's nearly two decades younger than Jack Weil, the 105-year-old top man at Rockmount Ranch Wear, a privately owned Western clothing company based in Denver). Melvin's wife, Ellen, a youthful 74, is president and chief operating officer. Neither shows any sign of an overindulged sweet tooth.

Melvin, reading from a script, gets through the agenda quickly. The votes are formalities, because the Gordons control more than 40 percent of the company's common stock (one vote per share) and more than 80 percent of the class B stock (ten votes per share).

Melvin has been with Tootsie Roll for half of its 110-year history, and his long-term perspective comes in handy when he tells us what's happening these days in the candy industry: "Consolidation is reducing bargaining opportunities. All the corn syrup suppliers raised their prices two-and-a-half percent this year, which is either some kind of collusion or else they're all thinking the same thing. What's your guess?"

He talks about how price increases for Tootsie Roll products will help the company's earnings. In some cases, the products themselves will be made smaller. (You can still buy penny Tootsie Rolls, but you might need a magnifying glass to see them.)

Of course, higher prices are just one way to make the company more profitable. Others, as Ellen points out, include acquiring other candy manufacturers, selling in more places, getting more mileage out of existing products, and—oh, yes—introducing *new* products. She smiles and says she has a lot of new products to tell us about today, and that we'll get to sample them all. Right away she mentions Cry Baby gumballs and shows us a big plastic jar full of them. Will's eyes just about pop out of his head, and he's a very happy young man when Ellen says he can have the whole jar.

Over and over again, Ellen reaches under the table and pulls out boxes and bags of wondrous treats like tangerine-mango Blow Pops and lime cola Tootsie Rolls, plus "limited edition" goodies, including caramel Tootsie Pops and chocolate-covered Sugar Babies. Perhaps the biggest news is that old favorites Sugar Babies and Sugar Daddy will be joined by Sugar Mamas ("and soon," Melvin jokes, "Sugar *Grandmothers*").

Each time, she rips open the box or bag and sends it on its way around the room, with everyone taking samples. I tuck mine in my briefcase, figuring it's too early in the day for all that candy. Also, if they're the only souvenirs, I don't want to leave here empty-handed.

All the while, she's pointing out improvements in packaging. Dubble Bubble gum, for instance, is now sold in a thick foil package that costs more to make but seems more substantial to consumers because it eliminates the floppy "dead fish syndrome" that is common with plastic packaging.

We're all still busying ourselves with the samples when Ellen asks if we have any questions. Andy's hand shoots into the air. He wants to know if Tootsie Roll has thought about merging with See's Candies. Ellen Gordon admits that she's fond of See's herself before gently explaining that it's owned outright by Berkshire Hathaway and not up for grabs.

A financial analyst asks how increasing public attention to eating well is affecting the company. "We believe strongly that candy and treats are a logical part of a healthy diet," Ellen responds without knocking on wood or winking, although it's possible she may have had her fingers crossed. "Of course, balance is necessary." Melvin jumps in with "We do some sugar-free stuff. And some Tootsie Rolls have milk and nutrition-like things in them." (Hmmm. I've got to start reading ingredient labels more carefully. *Nutrition-like things?*)

A man who says he's here to represent his eleven-year-old son's shares asks if the company has considered capitalizing on its appeal to children by creating an educational program for schools. "Actually, we've been doing one for fifteen years or so," Melvin says. "It's for second and third graders and stresses math and geography. We give them maps showing where our manufacturing plants are, and teach them how to make change based on Tootsie Roll purchases."

After the meeting ends, Will—who says he'd like to be an engineer someday—tells me he thought it was "pretty interesting, although I didn't understand some of the things they were saying." I assure him that's often the case for *adults* at most shareholder meetings.

His favorite part, he says, was when Ellen Gordon gave him the big jar of Cry Baby gumballs. "There are three hundred in there," he says, offering me one. "They should last a week!"

Chances are they'll survive a little longer than that, because as we shuffle to the elevator, a group of Tootsie Roll employees is waiting for us, cheerfully handing out the largest goodie bags I've seen yet. Mine includes full-size packages of a dozen different Tootsie Roll products, ranging from Andes Peppermint Chips for baking to the new Sugar Mama Caramels to gummy stalwart Dots (which my wife sold as a candy girl in an Ohio movie theater many years ago). Because there are more bags than shareholders, we're invited to take extras. Will's mom does, explaining that her son has three older sisters, all of whom are also shareholders.

Leaving the building, I catch up with young Andy Ross and his dad, Steve, a stockbroker who, it turns out, is a Warren Buffett fan and is headed for Omaha, as I am, later this week. Steve thinks the Tootsie Roll meeting and the Berkshire Hathaway meeting are similar. "There's no sugarcoating at either one," he says, then breaks into a grin when he recognizes his pun.

This isn't the first time Steve has been to Tootsie Roll's annual gathering. He brought Andy's sister, Jenna, six years ago. But this is the first shareholder meeting for Andy, who says he wants to be an architect when he grows up. What did he learn today? "You have to pay a lot for supplies, and there's a lot to know about shipping and packaging," he says. Was it worth taking a day off from school? Duh. "It was better than Halloween!"

Will feels the same way. "All I had to do is wear my spiffy shoes and I get a bag full of candy. It's a no-brainer!"

In a nutshell . . .

TOOTSIE ROLL

EDUCATIONAL VALUE: **B**
  A good "starter" for young investors.

ENTERTAINMENT VALUE: **A**
  "New products" taste test.

FREEBIES: **A+**
  Trick or treat!

FOOD & DRINK: **B**
  Sodas, coffee, candies.

INSIGHT: If you're investing on behalf of a child, consider choosing a stock with a natural appeal to a younger person. The company's shareholder meeting could be an unforgettably rewarding educational experience.

22

Geek No Evil

GOOGLE

Disclosure: Every once in a while, those limited partnerships I'd invested in ages ago would send me a few shares in a company I actually knew. In early 2005 I received some Google stock, because the venture capital outfit that managed the partnerships was among the original backers for the search firm whose very name has become a verb. Even though I was a longtime Googler by then, my instinct was to sell the shares—to get while the getting was good, as it were. But I was intrigued by the plain-English "Owner's Manual" the company issued when the stock was first publicly traded in 2004. In it, the founders said their motto was "Don't Be Evil" and vowed—some would say warned—in the very first sentence of the introduction that "Google is not a conventional company." Unlike its tech industry brethren, Google would focus on the long term. The message invoked Warren Buffett, and the founders made it clear they wanted to run Google much like Buffett runs Berkshire Hathaway. This I had to see.

East of the 101 Freeway in Mountain View, California—an hour south of San Francisco if traffic's light—there are dozens of shiny new buildings, each seemingly big enough to house one of the hundreds of high-tech companies based in the area. Yet each and every one I'm passing seems to have the same logo out front—six letters in primary colors on a white background: Google.

Fortunately, the place I'm supposed to park for Google's 2006 shareholder meeting is in the lot for Shoreline Amphitheatre. The fact that it *isn't* a Google facility helps make it relatively easy to find.

At a sign-in table under a white tarp, a team of smiling young Googlers checks brokerage statements for proof of share ownership before handing out clip-on badges and adhesive wristbands declaring all shareholders to be VIPs. It's a very warm welcome.

A Google shuttle bus takes us onto the campus known as the Googleplex (which was an early contender for the actual name of the company). The comfy van is from a fleet used to move employees around the Bay Area, and the driver tells us it's equipped with tray tables and wireless Internet access to help maximize productivity.

Among my fellow passengers is a guy who admits to being an employee of Microsoft—a company that in some categories has been losing ground to Google—and he seems as impressed as the rest of us. He says that he's never been to a shareholder meeting before and wants to see how one works. It seems somewhat more likely he's on a spying mission. If so, he won't see much. We're escorted from the van directly into the No-Name Cafe, one of five company cafeterias that keep Googlers well fed for free. Through big glass windows we can see a huge indoor/outdoor dining area where hundreds of employees are enjoying lunch, but to talk with any of them we would have to get past the two security guards blocking the door.

I'm sure the young people eating beyond the glass are fascinating and brilliant, and I should rue not being able to talk with them. But I've just realized that we're being offered one of the rarest and most highly coveted of all shareholder perks: a free lunch. The meeting notice didn't mention this, so I had grabbed a bite before arriving. Still, the buffet looks wonderful, and shareholders who have already partaken are singing its praises. Next thing I know I'm savoring a bowl of Sweet Potato Jalapeño Bisque and writing myself a note to Google the recipe ASAP.

Minutes later, nibbling on a piece of flourless chocolate cake, I'm watching a demo of Gmail—Google's highly regarded e-mail service. Since Gmail was introduced in April 2004, it's been available by invitation only and has developed something of an exclusive cachet. Sensing an opportunity, I ask the twenty-something young woman doing the demo if Google might be willing to extend an invitation to a little old shareholder like me. "Sure," she says. "Got a cell phone?" I hand her my bottom-of-the-line privacy intrusion device, and in short order she's sent me a text message that makes me an official Gmail user, able to take advantage of features including online message storage that's basically unlimited. I'm thrilled—until I turn around and find that all the other shareholders have disappeared. (Also until I get home and discover that *anyone* can give their cell phone number to Google and be "invited" to open a Gmail account.)

One of the security guards points me in the right direction. I climb a very wide set of metal steps and catch up with the crowd just in time to grab a souvenir metallic blue coffee thermos from a rapidly dwindling supply. The meeting room somehow seems like the sort of place where you might work on your boat, if you had one (and I don't, so it's hard to be sure). It's all clean, exposed metal—save for a carpet featuring bright orange circles on a field of black. The company logo is on three white screens at the front.

There are maybe two hundred shareholders here. Some are barely out of their teens, while others are senior citizens. I don't see the guy from Microsoft, but he may have disguised himself as a potted plant.

Eric Schmidt, chairman of the company, is one of the very few people present wearing a suit. He steps to the lectern and greets us enthusiastically: "This is *your* company and we're happy to have you here!" It's a refreshing sentiment and one I've seldom heard (or felt) anywhere other than at a Berkshire Hathaway meeting.

Schmidt, who's fifty, looks a little like Dennis the Menace—yet he's the resident "adult supervision" enabling founders Sergey Brin and Larry Page, both in their early thirties, to focus on the sorts of big ideas that have made Google a household word in a very short time. The company was founded a decade ago, when Brin and Page, then students at nearby Stanford University, created their intuitive search engine and established their preposterous goal of harnessing all the knowledge in the world.

By the time Google went public, it was answering approximately twenty-five hundred queries per second and had already been the world's leading search engine for several years. The IPO (initial public offering) was long awaited by investors who marveled at how Google's popularity led to phenomenal advertising revenues. Brin and Page had qualms about the usual IPO process, which involves high-paid investment bankers allocating the initial shares and setting an opening stock price. In theory, the price reflects expert opinions about the demand. Often, though, the price is set artificially low so that rabid investors who arrive once the party's already under way can drive it higher, enabling insiders to take quick profits at the expense of the newcomers. Google's founders insisted on a fairer approach and settled on a Dutch auction—where anyone could pick a price they would like to pay, and orders would be filled from most expensive on down, until all the shares to be issued were distributed. Wall Street didn't think much of that idea and began sniping at Google, casting aspersions on the relative maturity of Brin and Page and suggesting the two should be more "normal" if they knew what was good for them. The criticisms helped push the initial price for Google down from early estimates of as much as two hundred dollars a share to eighty-five dollars a share. Yet the founders had the last laugh. Within weeks the stock was trading at two hundred dollars, and less than a year later it broached four hundred dollars.

"I'll try to dispense with the formal part of the meeting quickly," Schmidt says, "so we can get to the more interesting stuff, and I hope we'll have vigorous and exciting debate. By the way, we hope you enjoyed the food!" The applause leaves no doubt.

Schmidt introduces the company's executives and members of its board. When he gets to Brin and Page, he laughs and says with obvious affection, "What can you say about the founders?" Brin (president of technology) and Page (president of products) are sitting in the front row, and Brin's wearing a black T-shirt. He looks even more comfortable than the Hawaiian Electric executives did in their Hawaiian shirts.

The formal nominations of directors and auditors and the amendment of a stock option plan are fast and painless, which takes us to the only other bit of official business—a shareholder proposal seeking to eliminate Google's two-tiered share class system, which is similar to the one at Tootsie Roll. Jake McIntyre, a thirtyish representative of the Bricklayers and Trowel Trades International Pension Fund, makes the case that a company known for its "remarkably democratic software" shouldn't be structured in such a way that the founders have "supervoting" shares that are more potent than mere mortal shares (like mine).

McIntyre spends the first of his three minutes praising the company and establishing that he's "not standing in opposition to Google." He takes a cue from Google itself and keeps his presentation simple and friendly, even referring to Brin and Page as "Sergey" and "Larry" as he chides them for having 66 percent of the voting power while holding 31 percent of the company's stock. "It's ironic," McIntyre notes, "that a company that has built its success on the wisdom of crowds does not respect the wisdom of its shareholders."

When this issue has come up at the meetings of newspaper publishers, including the *New York Times* and Dow Jones, the media outlets have said their independence is dependent on keeping voting power to a very small group of shareholders—typically the founders and/or their relatives. It's a dichotomy as proposals go, because unless the very people who hold the power agree with the presentation—not likely—there's no chance of success. So much, once again, for shareholder democracy.

McIntyre closes by admitting, "We know we're not going to win today, but we wanted to get this issue on the table."

He's right. A minute or so later the preliminary vote totals are announced and there are no surprises.

I realize that I've seen union people at maybe a third of the meetings I've attended. Most of the time they've been representing current or former employees of the company hosting the gathering, and they've had a bone to pick about labor relations. That was the case at Hershey and DuPont, for example. At Citigroup's meeting and now here at Google's, the unions have focused on investor issues, looking out for the assets of union pension funds. Later I talk with McIntyre and he points out the obvious: unions are "a class of people that are, to some degree, activists."

As Schmidt prepares to talk about the current state of things at Google, a daunting message appears on one of the screens at the front of the room. The big type at the top says "A Note From Our Lawyers," and it's followed by lots of little type—all legible but not very inviting. Schmidt gets a gleam in his eye and teases, "I can read this to you . . . ," leaving unspoken, "*or?*" We all laugh as he pauses for a second or two before asking, "Has everyone read it?" and moving on.

"I don't remember a time before I had Google to answer all the wacky questions," Schmidt begins, telling us how much he admired the company even before he came aboard in 2001. He praises Brin and Page for their foresight, noting that they understood "the idea of putting together information and monetizing it. The [Silicon] Valley is full of people who got one of those things right."

Google makes money—lots of it—by selling advertisements that are so unobtrusive many users say they don't even see them. But the huge number of Google users means that "plenty of people do see the ads, click on them, and order products," Schmidt says. While the clean look of a Google search page is one reason why ads seem to blend in so well, what's most important is that ads displayed are targeted to the user. If you've just run a search for information about, say, tongue depressors for left-handers, the right side of the results screen will include

simple ads from several vendors offering—surprise!—
tongue depressors for left-handers.

Unlike almost every other corporate executive I've
heard, Schmidt avoids double-talk. It isn't until several
minutes into his presentation that Schmidt uses any tech
lingo at all, and even then it's only to describe something
as "mission critical." Yet there's no hint of condescension.
Meanwhile, he reinforces the warm welcome we received
by continuing to call Google "your company" and telling
us "we're very happy to have you all be a part of it!"

He seems very happy, period—like a man who loves his
job (reminiscent of Buffett, who says he "tap dances to
work"). From the way he tells the tale, Schmidt's so happy
at work that he prefers virtual vacations to real ones. He
says he likes to use Google Earth, which combines aerial
and satellite photos (all taken in the past three years) to provide a detailed online globe, to circle the planet and swoop
in here and there for a closer look. "It's much easier to take
Google Earth to go to Mount Everest than it is to actually
go to Mount Everest," Schmidt observes. (Obviously he
doesn't have a dial-up Internet connection, like I do.)

Schmidt tells us that ideas like Google Earth come from
the company's "20 percent time" policy. Employees are
expected to spend 20 percent of their time doing activities
other than what they've been assigned—in short, creating
clever things. "Half the ideas that come out of the exercise
are bad," Schmidt admits. "We just don't know which half!"
So does the policy mean that Google employees can spend
the equivalent of one standard workday each week goofing
off? Nope. "You have to remember," Schmidt notes with a
grin, "that the kind of people who work at Google work
one hundred hours a week anyway!"

There are a lot of people working at Google—more

than seven thousand as of March 2006 (more than one thousand of them added during the previous quarter alone). Little wonder Schmidt says confidently, "We have lots more stuff coming."

With that, it's Q&A time. Schmidt remains standing as Brin and Page move to a pair of directors' chairs facing the audience, flanked by CFO George Reyes and general counsel David Drummond. As everyone's settling in, Schmidt asks the group what the most important thing is about Picasa, the company's photo search program. Reyes takes a stab, suggesting it offers more results. "No!" Schmidt says, sounding a bit like John McLaughlin, the opinionated host of TV's *McLaughlin Group*, shooting down a guest's opinion. "The most important thing is that it's *free!*" Suddenly I understand why I have a warm and fuzzy feeling about Google while Microsoft leaves me cold, even though both have been known to release half-baked beta programs that aren't really ready for prime time. Unlike Microsoft, Google doesn't charge me to be a guinea pig!

The very first shareholder question takes us to a place where Google's leaders can prove whether they're really in synch with Warren Buffett. "Why don't you split the shares?" asks a shareholder. It's a fair question, given that the share price is around four hundred dollars. Many companies tend to do stock splits when the price tops fifty dollars or so, to keep shares "affordable" for smaller investors. Brin's answer sounds like a few I've heard in Omaha: "Having our stock price outside 'normal' trading ranges encourages people to look at the actual number of shares outstanding. We'd rather not have people thinking, 'Oh, it's twenty dollars a share; I'll buy it,' without doing the analysis."

A shareholder dandily dressed in white, like Tom Wolfe, announces that he's from Los Angeles and has a complaint about how Google deals with the media. The company hosted a press day here yesterday, and today's papers quoted Brin as calling Microsoft a "convicted monopoly." That doesn't sit well with the shareholder, who grouses, "Every time an executive from Google says something, it's negative. This morning I was down thirty thousand dollars by seven fifteen!" Schmidt responds, "We can't control the press. We just think it's better from a business perspective to tell people what's up." Again, it's reminiscent of Buffett.

There's been plenty of newspaper coverage recently of Google's efforts in China, where the company gave in to government pressure and created a site (google.cn) that withholds certain search results. A representative of Amnesty International stands and says Google is "a partner with an oppressive regime." Brin asks the shareholder, "Which search engine do you use?" When it turns out to be Yahoo! Brin raises an eyebrow and continues, "You mean the one that's been censoring since the nineties?" A bit red-faced, the shareholder responds, "Yes, and believe me, we've got Yahoo! lined up, too." Brin turns on the charm and admits the situation is less than perfect, then lauds the shareholder for being here and caring about the issue. Page points out that one way Google has tried to do the right thing in China is by telling google.cn users that search results can be incomplete because of censorship issues. At this point, the Amnesty International guy is nodding.

"What are we being sued for these days?" another shareholder wants to know. Drummond, the company lawyer, doesn't dodge the question: "A variety of things. We run into a lot of areas where our innovation puts us up against laws not designed for the world we live in—the digital world." One of those areas, of course, is book publishing. Google, in pursuit of its mission to gather all the world's information and put it at everyone's fingertips, has been trying to find ways to put entire libraries online without violating the rights of authors and publishers.

Meanwhile, the company has refused to comply with a government subpoena to provide detailed records of searches by Google users. Instead, it got a federal judge to agree that a list of searches—not associated with any user information— would suffice. "The government asked for lots and lots of information we didn't think was appropriate. You can count on us to do that sort of thing," Drummond tells an audience so appreciative it gives him a round of applause.

A relaxed middle-aged guy stands and says, "I've got my life's savings in Google, so I took a day off to check up on my four shares." When the laughter ends, he asks his question: "What will the world be like in five years?" It's exactly the sort of Really Big Question people like to ask Warren Buffett. Schmidt says technology will be faster, cheaper, and better. He pauses for a minute, then talks about a conversation he'd had with Brin, who had told him that someday "it'd be great to make the final connection—a direct connection to your brain." Schmidt says that at the time, he had responded with "Gimme a break!" Now he turns to Brin and says, "Sergey, are you still thinking of that?" Brin smiles and answers, "Sure, if you're willing to go first!" The banter would do Buffett and Charlie Munger proud.

A week or so later, when I sit down to write this chapter and wrap up my shareholder meeting odyssey, I wonder how my account of Google's gathering meshes with news stories and online postings. So I Google "Google" and "shareholder meetings" and make a discovery that astonishes me: There's a real-time blog of the meeting (on bloggingstocks.com)! How could I have overlooked someone who was apparently sitting in the room, tapping away on a keyboard—or maybe even thumbing furiously to update the blog with text messages? As I read on, the blog turns out to be a tag-team effort, so not catching the contributors in the act baffles me even more. Finally, I realize the writers weren't actually at the meeting itself: They were listening to the Web cast.

That, I think, is why they say they're underwhelmed— they're *ear*witnesses, not *eye*witnesses. Being there can make a big difference in what you see, hear, and take away (figuratively and literally).

In a nutshell . . .

GOOGLE

EDUCATIONAL VALUE: **B+**
 An interesting glimpse of the corporate culture.

ENTERTAINMENT VALUE: **B+**
 Product demos, no song and dance.

FREEBIES: **B**
 Attractive coffee thermos with Google logo.

FOOD & DRINK: **A+**
 Lunch in Google's superb cafeteria!

INSIGHT: In the animated comedy *South Park: Bigger, Longer and Uncut*, a contemplative Satan sings, "Without evil there could be no good, so it must be good to be evil sometimes." It's a clever line, but I'd prefer my world evil-free, thanks. So would the folks at Google, and that comes through loud and clear in their warmth and honesty on shareholder meeting day.

EPILOGUE

One of the reasons to visit Omaha during the first weekend in May used to be "Berkshire Hathaway Night" at the local ballpark, when Warren Buffett would don a uniform and throw out the ceremonial first pitch. He would joke that his fastball had been clocked at nineteen miles an hour, but he never embarrassed himself out there. Afterward, he would take a seat in the stands and sign autographs for a never-ending stream of admirers.

Buffett hung up his cleats after the 2002 season, and now the big Saturday night event is a barbeque under a huge tent in the parking lot of Nebraska Furniture, one of Berkshire's hometown subsidiaries. Buffett makes only a token appearance. He drives a 2006 Cadillac these days, which he bought after publicly admiring the way that Rick Wagoner, chairman and CEO of struggling General Motors, handled a tough TV interview.

It's a safe bet he's lost a little speed on his fastball. His wife, Susie, died in 2004; although they had lived separately for many years, they remained close and she was the second-largest holder of Berkshire Hathaway shares. Meanwhile, New York State attorney general Eliot Spitzer's investigation of the insurance industry uncovered a few questionable deals involving Berkshire subsidiaries. Nobody questions Buffett's integrity, which has long been considered beyond reproach.

Since 2004 the shareholder meeting has been held in shiny new Qwest Arena, the only place in town able to accommodate such a large crowd (an estimated twenty-four thousand in 2006). While both Buffett and Munger sometimes sound a little weary, they continue to share their wit and wisdom and everyone has a wonderful time. I sure do. (Some see the meeting as a religious experience, including, in 2006, one long-winded shareholder from India who told Buffett, "I'm waiting for my chance to touch your feet and get your blessing.")

In 2005 Buffett moved the business meeting to the very end of the day, explaining that not many people want to sit through shareholder proposals. That may be true, but presentations of proposals seldom take more than a few minutes, and investors jump through considerable hoops to make them. So it's possible Buffett is effectively silencing dissent—not the sort of thing I would expect from him.

I still feel like I learn something new every year. In 2006 one of my favorite insights came when a shareholder asked how Buffett reconciles his distaste for gambling with owning insurance companies that effectively place bets on risks. Buffett's answer seemed perfect: "Gambling involves creating risks that don't need to be created, whereas if you've got a home or a business in a coastal area, for example, the risk is already there and the question is, who bears it." (Only later did I remember that in 2003 Berkshire Hathaway underwrote a policy for a Pepsi contest with a long-shot grand prize of $1 billion.)

I decided, in 2006, to try to be one of the three dozen or so people who spent a brief moment in the spotlight, asking a question of Buffett and Munger. So when the doors opened, I made a beeline for the seats near one of the twelve microphones. I nabbed the third chair and was told by a staffer the odds were very good that I'd get to ask my question. Before the meeting began, I talked with the two guys in front of me—a British father and son. The son, Euen Gunn, a scientist with Johnson & Johnson, had snagged the first chair, and it wasn't long before he was standing at the microphone, leading into a relatively complicated investment question by admitting to a case of nerves most people would have shared, given the size of the audience. "The last time I was this nervous asking a question," he says, "was when I proposed to my wife after giving her a diamond from Borsheim's!" As the morning wore on, I grew more and more confident that no one would ask my question: "What can a shareholder meeting tell investors about a company?" And no one did. But somehow Buffett answered it anyway, while addressing a query about how managers are trained at Berkshire companies. He observed that the annual report and the annual meeting are handled the way they are for a reason. "This meeting is intended to give a personality and a character to Berkshire. We don't think it's better than anyone else's. A business has a culture, and we try to do everything that's consistent with that and nothing that's inconsistent with that." I abandoned my place in line and headed downstairs to see what sort of samples See's was giving away. There were none that I could find. In fact, the freebies seem to have dried up altogether in Omaha. I didn't see even one in 2006.

The energy's still there, though. When Buffett wrapped up the Q&A, I half expected to see the crowd hold lighters aloft and refuse to leave the auditorium without a few encores.

A month or so later Buffett wowed the world by announcing a plan to begin distributing his fortune— approximately $42 billion, according to *Forbes*. The vast majority of the money will go to the Bill & Melinda Gates Foundation, which focuses largely on global health problems. It will effectively double the assets of the foundation. Buffett, talking about what led him to make the remarkable gift, observed that he has a knack for making money but his friends Bill and Melinda are better at putting it to work for the greater good.

In August 2006 Buffett married Astrid Menks, his longtime companion.

Here's what's happened at some of the other companies in this book since I visited their shareholder meetings:

■ Starbucks has continued to grow like kudzu, and there are now ten thousand-plus stores in more than thirty countries plus all fifty states (although the company's annual report and Web site still don't include Hawaii as part of the United States). Orin Smith has retired as president and CEO. Meanwhile, I've become a coffee drinker. Rarely do more than a few days pass without a visit to Starbucks, where I've never had a bad cup. The stock has proved to be one of the best investments I've ever made, up more than fivefold since 1999. To hear the company tell it, there's still plenty of potential: At the 2006 shareholder meeting, Tony Bennett sang "The Best Is Yet to Come."

■ Otter Tail has sold its minor league baseball team subsidiary, the Redhawks, to a group of private investors headed by Bruce Thom (who left the company) and added, of all things, a potato processing company to its holdings. I bought more shares in 2003. The Otter Tail pocket date book I got at the shareholder meeting turned out to be indispensable, and every year I take advantage of the company's offer to send me a new one. The stock price hasn't moved much for a few years, but the yield—typically in the neighborhood of 4 percent—has been a nice reward for patience.

■ Hershey's employees went back to work in 2002 after forty-four days, agreeing to accept a lower wage increase in exchange for the company not lowering medical plan contributions. Shortly afterward, the company put itself up for sale and then changed its mind. I sold my shares when the price jumped at the announcement of a possible sale. Since then the stock has more or less doubled. Oh, well—it seemed like a good idea at the time. Meanwhile, CEO Richard Lenny has made good on his promise to add a sugar-free product line. And inflatable beasts have continued to turn up as protest props at shareholder meetings: in 2006 a group that accused Wells Fargo of predatory loan practices drew attention to their point with several dozen helium-filled sharks.

■ Newspapers have continued to lose readers to the Internet, and Gannett's results have been in red ink for several years. I sold my shares in mid-2005, which was right around when Evelyn Davis married a man who had sent her three fan letters. It was her fourth marriage; unfortunately, it ended in divorce a year later. Doug McCorkindale stepped down as CEO of Gannett in 2005 and retired as chairman in 2006.

■ At V-One hoped-for government contracts never came through—perhaps due to turf wars among various security agencies that might have benefited by using the company's software to share files. V-One hung on until spring 2005, when it was acquired by privately held AEP Networks, a New Jersey–based Internet security firm.

■ Hawaiian Electric CEO and president Robert Clarke retired in 2006 and was replaced by Connie Lau, who had been running the company's American Savings Bank subsidiary. I still haven't learned how to play the ukulele.

■ Hugh Hefner turned eighty in 2006, the same year that his current girlfriends turned twenty-one, twenty-seven, and thirty-three. It turns out I'm quite wrong about anyone being interested in the quartet's exploits, now featured in a very popular E! network show called *The Girls Next Door.* Jim Kaminsky lasted less than a year and a half as editor of *Playboy* magazine.

■ I sold my shares in Wal-Mart in 2004 as the company battled charges of sexual discrimination and inadequate employee benefits. Tom Coughlin, the number two man, resigned in 2005 amid accusations of misappropriating company funds; in 2006 he was sentenced to twenty-seven months of home confinement. The company's 2006 shareholder meeting featured two dozen New York actors performing a ninety-minute musical comedy about working at Wal-Mart, complete with choreographed dance routines involving shopping carts.

■ In 2004 Microsoft treated shareholders to the largest special dividend payout of all time. Yet in mid-2006 the company still had a whopping $35 billion in cash (all by itself an amount larger than the total assets of all but one hundred or so public U.S. companies), and CEO Steve Ballmer was telling investors that the company needed the money to explore new technologies. Meanwhile, the much-touted Longhorn operating system has been renamed Vista, and the estimated release date is now early 2007. Bill Gates has announced he plans to get out of the company's day-to-day operations loop in 2008 and become a full-time philanthropist. Thanks to his friend Warren Buffett, he'll have even more money to help fight global health scourges. I traded my PC for a Mac a few years ago, so I no longer spend much of my time debugging and defragging.

■ In 2004 I used my Bowl America gift card to bowl a few games and discovered that just because I was reasonably good at something once didn't mean I always would be. In early 2005 Bowl America was dropped from the Mergent Dividend Achiever's list—which recognizes companies that have raised their dividends for at least ten consecutive years—because the company is so thinly traded. I bought a few more shares in late 2005, and my purchase marked the only Bowl America stock transaction that day.

■ Michael Eisner stepped down as Disney's CEO in 2005, and the company adopted a policy that requires board nominees to receive a majority of votes cast. Under Robert Iger, Eisner's successor, Disney purchased Pixar Animation Studios from Apple founder and CEO Steve Jobs, who now sits on Disney's board of directors. Eisner now hosts a celebrity talk show on CNBC. I sold my Disney shares right after the 2004 meeting. The stock price hasn't changed much since then.

■ DuPont placed first on *BusinessWeek*'s 2005 list of "The Top Green Companies" and was lauded by the magazine for greatly reducing the amount of air pollution it creates. In mid-2006 DuPont announced plans to reduce something else—employee pension benefits. As with Disney, I bought my shares before the 2004 shareholder meeting and sold them shortly afterward, and the stock price has stayed about the same.

■ MGM Mirage has continued to be a good bet for investors, with the share price nearly doubling since I went to the 2004 shareholder meeting. Later that year it gobbled up the Mandalay Resort Group—more than a dozen properties, including such Vegas landmarks as Mandalay Bay Resort and Casino, Luxor, and Circus Circus. In 2006 the Boardwalk casino— the only one where I had gone zero for ten dollars— was closed as part of preparations for Project CityCenter, described in the company's 2005 annual report as "18 million square feet of resort, convention, retail and residential space, far larger than any privately funded development in our nation's history." During a quick visit to Las Vegas in August 2006, I savored "Love," a Cirque du Soleil spectacular set to Beatles music; the show is reinvigorating the Mirage. I also discovered that many twenty-five-cent slot machines no longer accept coins at all! (You need to feed them dollar bills.)

■ Former Chalone shareholders, bought out by Diageo, were invited to join "The Founder's Club." Those who did continue to enjoy periodic wine discounts and invitations to the annual feast (where attendance fell to five hundred or so in 2006). Tom Selfridge left Chalone after the takeover and is now president of the Hess Collection, a Napa Valley winery.

■ In 2005 eBay's stock was pummeled. So was New Orleans, ravaged by Hurricane Katrina. Thousands displaced from their homes took uneasy shelter in the huge convention center where I had attended eBay Live! While some parts of the city—notably the French Quarter—were largely unscathed by the effects of the storm and the subsequent flooding, the convention center sustained a great deal of damage and as of mid-2006 it had only been partially restored. The eBay Live! event was held in Washington, D.C., in 2005 and Las Vegas in 2006.

■ In June 2006 Ansell terminated its ADR program, which represented just half of 1 percent of the company's total outstanding shares. ADR holders were allowed to receive ordinary shares (traded on the Australian market) or cash. Sadly, Ansell's chairman, Dr. Ed Tweddell, passed away in August 2005.

■ Dow Jones introduced a Saturday edition of the *Wall Street Journal* in fall 2005. I sold the stock a few months before that, not long after the shareholder meeting. Peter Kann resigned as CEO in January 2006, amid reports that the family that controls Dow Jones was unhappy with the company's lackluster financial results. Although my unsolicited advice to temper the *Journal*'s editorial page has gone unheeded, I now enjoy the rest of the paper six days a week.

■ Intercontinental Hotels Group held yet another "extraordinary shareholder meeting" in 2006, this time because the company had sold off its Britvic beverages division. Shareholders approved distributing the cash via a special dividend and a seven-shares-for-eight stock split intended to maintain the price after the dividend is paid. I will probably end up holding my shares forever, as I've given up all hope of ever calculating my actual cost basis. Also in 2006 the company eliminated the "show of hands" voting convention and moved to the American approach—where any ballots cast at the meeting are on paper and each share counts as one vote.

APPENDIX 1

WANT TO GO TO A
SHAREHOLDER MEETING?

HOW TO FIND OUT WHEN AND WHERE THE MEETING WILL
BE HELD:

■ Some companies (not many!) hold their meetings on the same day
and in the same place each year.

■ The best place to start looking for information is on the company's
Web site. Sometimes the meeting information will be posted right on
the Investor Relations page. More often, though, you'll have to dig
deeper. If there's no tab labeled "Proxy" or "Annual Meeting," look
for one labeled "SEC Filings." Click on it and look for the most
recent proxy statement, a document known as "DEF 14-A." It's the
proxy statement and meeting announcement you will eventually
receive, if you're a shareholder. If you don't find a DEF 14-A for the
current year, move backward until you find the previous year's document. In most instances, that will give you a reasonable idea when this
year's meeting might be held.

■ A few weeks in advance of the meeting itself, you should receive the
meeting notice and proxy statement, distributed with the company's
annual financial report. Sometimes the meeting materials are actually
included inside the report, which can save the company money. Typically, though, the meeting notice and proxy statement are a separate
brochure that often looks like a legal document (which it is). There
are some exceptions. The brochures produced by California Water
Service and First National Bank Alaska, for example, are colorful
companions designed to match the company's annual report. So are
BP's, which are even written in plain English, spelling out what visitors to the meeting can expect.

IF YOU HOLD AMERICAN DEPOSITARY RECEIPTS:

■ The underlying shares for your ADRs are actually owned by a custodian bank. The SEC doesn't require foreign companies to provide ADR holders with annual reports and proxy statements. Companies whose ADRs are listed on the New York Stock Exchange must deliver the materials to comply with NYSE rules, but as of mid-2006 the exchange was considering elimination of the requirement. In any case, if you really want to attend a shareholder meeting overseas it's best not to wait for the details to show up in your mailbox, because the wait might be too long. By the time you get your invitation to the shareholder meeting for, say, the phone company in Sri Lanka, the meeting may very well have already occurred.

■ Send an e-mail to the investor relations people at the company whose meeting you would like to attend. Chances are they'll be happy to have you visit. If there's any question whether the meeting will be conducted in a language you speak, ask.

■ If you wish to vote at the meeting, contact the custodian bank for your ADRs well in advance to see if it might be possible for it to give you a proxy to vote the underlying shares. Don't be surprised if the answer is no.

IF YOU DON'T RECEIVE THE MEETING INFORMATION IN THE MAIL:

■ Companies are required to provide brokerage firms with sufficient copies to mail to shareholders. Current SEC standards call for delivery of hard copies by the U.S. Postal Service unless you have indicated you would rather have the materials come to you electronically (via e-mail). If your mail carrier doesn't bring the information you're expecting, call your broker (or the company itself if you hold actual share certificates).

■ Perhaps you have authorized electronic delivery. That's fine if you check your e-mail regularly, and if you remember to let everyone know if you change your e-mail address, and if the materials survive your spam filters.

■ As this book was being completed, the U.S. Securities and Exchange Commission was considering changing the default to electronic delivery. Critics of such a change note that older folks, who are more likely to own stocks, tend to be among the least likely to use computers. Indeed, according to a January 2006 study by AARP, nearly half of those over age seventy don't have access to a personal computer, and nearly 40 percent of all investors at or near retirement age said they would be less likely to read documents delivered electronically than those that come in the mail. If the SEC makes the switch, investors will still be able to receive printed copies, but only by requesting them each and every year from each and every company whose shares they hold— a cumbersome process, at best.

IF YOU DON'T ACTUALLY OWN ANY SHARES:

■ Contact the company's investor relations department and ask if you might be allowed to attend as a guest of the company. Warning: Odds are good the investor relations folks may not return your calls. (Actually, that's true even if you do own some shares.)

■ If a friend or relative owns shares and attends the meeting, you might be able to attend as his or her guest.

■ If you know a shareholder who does not plan to attend, see if he or she would be willing to give you his or her proxy.

■ Many companies are pretty loose at the front door and don't check statements or ID. Consider just showing up and looking like you belong.

IN ANY CASE:

■ Read the meeting announcement carefully to see if there are any special requirements, such as requesting an admission ticket in advance.

Sometimes the stub from the ballot that's enclosed with the proxy statement serves as an admission ticket. (The proxy statement, by the way, includes quite a bit of information about the company, including details about how much the executives get paid, backgrounds of the directors, and arguments for and against issues up for a vote by shareholders.)

■ If you would like to bring your spouse or another guest and the invitation isn't clear about whether that's okay, contact the company's investor relations department for clarification.

■ Unless you hold actual share certificates, be sure to bring a copy of the brokerage statement proving you owned shares in the company as of the "record date" cited in the proxy statement. For privacy's sake, consider running a thick black line through your account number and any other personal information.

■ Bring a photo ID.

■ Keep in mind that there's no guarantee they'll let you in, even if you are a shareholder. In 2000, for instance, Pepsico banned a shareholder who planned to speak against the company's ads being placed in bull-fight rings.

■ Remember that the shareholder meeting "season" in the United States is April and May. So if you want to go to several companies' meetings, you might be dismayed to learn they're all happening on the same day, in different parts of the country.

■ Unless you're an investment professional, don't even think about trying to take a tax deduction for your expenses attending a shareholder meeting.

IF YOU WANT TO ASK A QUESTION AT THE MEETING:

■ As you enter the meeting room, look for microphones in or near aisles. Sit near one!

■ If there's a staff person who seems to be in charge of coordinating questions from the audience, check in with him or her to maximize the chances you'll be called on.

■ Think your question through so you can be succinct when the time comes.

■ Before asking your question, tell everyone who you are and what your primary interest is in the company (shareholder, customer, supplier, employee, etc.).

IF YOU WANT TO CAST YOUR BALLOT:

■ You can vote at the meeting itself, although almost no one does. The person running the meeting will ask if anyone needs a ballot. Raise your hand!

■ Before the meeting, follow the ballot instructions in the proxy statement. If you mail your ballot in the postage-paid envelope enclosed with a hard copy of a proxy statement, you'll almost certainly be sending it to P.O. Box 9138 in Farmingdale, New York (a Long Island town otherwise known only for how in 1899 a man there named Charles Murphy proved he could ride his bike nearly sixty miles per hour in the slipstream of a railroad train). The Farmingdale address is for Automatic Data Processing, which sends out materials announcing about thirteen thousand shareholder meetings each year. ADP says 90 percent of recipients read the materials and 45 percent vote. (That's remarkable, considering that only about half of all eligible voters cast their ballots in U.S. presidential elections!)

■ Even if you receive your materials in the mail, you can use the Internet to cast your vote.

■ Remember that if you're an individual investor in the Average Joe or Jane category, your vote probably doesn't amount to a hill of beans.

Institutional investors own the lion's share of most companies these days, and they have a lot more votes than you do. (What's more, many are fiduciaries—responsible for investing money held in trust for others and legally bound to vote the shares.)

IF YOU DON'T CAST YOUR BALLOT:

■ For "routine" matters, shares in a brokerage account can be voted however the brokerage firm chooses—and that tends to mean they'll be voted exactly as the company's management suggests. (Director elections are considered "routine" at this writing, but that may not be the case by the time this book is published.)

APPENDIX 2

DATES AND LOCATIONS OF MEETINGS
FEATURED IN THIS BOOK

ANSELL

October 14, 2004 (Melbourne Exhibition Centre, Melbourne, Australia)

BERKSHIRE HATHAWAY

May 5–7, 2006 (Qwest Center, Omaha)

April 29–May 1, 2005 (Qwest Center, Omaha)

April 30–May 2, 2004 (Qwest Center, Omaha)

May 2–4, 2003 (Omaha Civic Center)

May 3–5, 2002 (Omaha Civic Center)

April 27–29, 2001 (Omaha Civic Center)

April 28–30, 2000 (Omaha Civic Center)

May 1–3, 1999 (Aksarben Coliseum, Omaha)

BHP BILLITON

October 24, 2004 (Sydney Convention & Exhibition Centre, Sydney, Australia)

BOWL AMERICA

December 2, 2003 (Corporate headquarters, Alexandria, VA)

CHALONE WINE GROUP

May 15, 2004 (Chalone Vineyards, near Soledad, CA)

CITIGROUP

April 18, 2006 (Carnegie Hall, New York City)

DOW JONES

April 20, 2005 (Museum of the American Indian, New York City)

DUPONT

April 28, 2004 (DuPont Theatre, Wilmington, DE)

EBAY

June 24, 2004 (New Orleans Hilton, New Orleans)

GANNETT

May 7, 2002 (Frank Gannett Auditorium, McLean, VA)

GOOGLE

May 11, 2006 (The Googleplex, Mountain View, CA)

HAWAIIAN ELECTRIC

April 22, 2003 (American Savings Bank Tower, Honolulu)

HERSHEY

April 30, 2002 (Hershey Theater, Hershey, PA)

INTERCONTINENTAL HOTELS

June 1, 2005 (Queen Elizabeth II Convention Centre, London, England)

MGM MIRAGE

May 11, 2004 (New York–New York Hotel and Casino, Las Vegas, NV)

MICROSOFT

November 11, 2003 (Meydenbauer Center, Bellevue, WA)

OTTER TAIL

April 8, 2002 (Bigwood Event Center, Fergus Falls, MN)

PLAYBOY

May 14, 2003 (Spiaggia Club, Chicago)

STARBUCKS

February 22, 2002 (Benaroya Hall, Seattle, WA)

TOOTSIE ROLL

May 1, 2006 (Mutual Building, Richmond, VA)

V-ONE

May 16, 2002 (Glenview Mansion, Rockville Civic Center, Rockville, MD)

WAL-MART

June 6, 2003 (Bud Walton Arena, University of Arkansas, Fayetteville, AR)

WALT DISNEY

March 2, 2004 (Pennsylvania Convention Center, Philadelphia, PA)

Appendix 3

Suggestions for Further Reading

Anderson, Chris. *The Long Tail: Why the Future of Businesses Is Selling Less of More*. New York: Hyperion, 2006.

Carlson, Charles B. *Free Lunch on Wall Street: Perks, Freebies, and Giveaways for Investors*. New York: McGraw-Hill, 1993.

Court, Jamie. *Corporateering: How Corporate Power Steals Your Personal Freedom . . . And What You Can Do About It*. New York: Jeremy P. Tarcher/Putnam, 2003.

Domini, Amy. *Socially Responsible Investing: Making a Difference and Making Money*. Chicago: Dearborn Trade, 2001.

Gilbert, Lewis D. *Dividends and Democracy*. Larchmont, NY: American Research Council, 1956.

Graham, Benjamin. *The Intelligent Investor: The Definitive Book on Value Investing*. (Rev. ed., updated with new commentary by Jason Zweig). New York: HarperBusiness Essentials, 2003.

Hagstrom, Robert G. *The Essential Buffett: Timeless Principles for the New Economy*. New York: Wiley, 2001.

Kaufman, Peter D. *Poor Charlie's Almanack: The Wit and Wisdom of Charles T. Munger*. Marceline, MO: Walsworth, 2005.

Kilpatrick, Andy. *Of Permanent Value: The Story of Warren Buffett*. Birmingham, AL: AKPE Financial Center, 2006.

Lowe, Janet. *Damn Right! Behind the Scenes with Berkshire Hathaway Billionaire Charlie Munger*. New York: Wiley, 2000.

———. *Warren Buffett Speaks: Wit and Wisdom from the World's Greatest Investor*. New York: Wiley, 1997.

Lowenstein, Roger. *Buffett: The Making of an American Capitalist*. New York: Random House, 1995.

Mahoney, William F. *The Active Shareholder: Exercising Your Rights, Increasing Your Profits, and Minimizing Your Risks.* New York: Wiley, 1993.

Morio, Ayano. *Warren Buffett: An Illustrated Biography of the World's Most Successful Investor.* Singapore: Wiley (Asia), 2003.

Prindle, Tamae K. *Made In Japan and Other Japanese "Business Novels."* Armonk, NY: M. E. Sharpe, 1999.

Rittenhouse, L. J. *Do Business with People You Can Trust: Balancing Profits and Principles.* New York: andBEYOND Communications, 2002.

Slater, Robert. *The Wal-Mart Decade: How a New Generation of Leaders Turned Sam Walton's Legacy into the World's #1 Company.* New York: Penguin, 2003.

Talner, Lauren. *The Origins of Shareholder Activism.* Washington, DC: Investor Responsibility Research Center, 1983.

Tilburn, Jack. *Corporate Terminator.* Self-published: Sydney, 2002.

Vise, David A. *The Google Story.* New York: Delacorte Press, 2005.

Woodward, W. Philip, and Gregory S. Walter. *Chalone: A Journey on the Wine Frontier.* Sonoma, CA: Carneros Press, 2000.

ACKNOWLEDGMENTS

While researching and writing this book, I had the pleasure of talking with, learning from, and enjoying the company of many wonderful people—more than there is space to recognize here.

Among those most gracious with their time and expertise (and not mentioned elsewhere in this book) were several old friends and colleagues from my American Funds years: Mike Downer, Deb Eppolito, Paul Haaga, Joe Higdon, Jim Ryan, and Parker Simes. Their financial industry insights were invaluable. Similarly crucial were Carol Bowie of Institutional Shareholder Services, Chuck Callan of ADP, and Richard Koppes of Jones Day, as well as Paul Maddock and Anthony O'Shea of MLC.

Joy Tutela, my agent, patiently introduced me to the ways of the publishing world, and I greatly appreciate her unwavering confidence. The folks at Thunder's Mouth Press have been wonderfully supportive: John Oakes and Michele Martin saw the book's potential, while Lukas Volger, Peter Jacoby, Jill Hughes, and Lori Lewis massaged my manuscript with great care and have done their considerable best to make the most of it.

Special thanks go to Scott Sparling, my longtime friend and an outstanding writer, for his boundless enthusiasm and superb editorial suggestions.

Others whose kind words, inspiring practices, creative thoughts, and/or generous hospitality helped make this book possible include Bruce Bacon, Jan and Kathi Fedor, Kathleen Hesse, Becky Lynch-Bacon, Lewis Shuster, and my parents.

Most of all, I'm grateful to my wife, Nancy, for believing in this book and encouraging me to write it ever since I first mentioned the idea five years ago.